SCRIPTWORK

A DIRECTOR'S APPROACH TO
NEW PLAY DEVELOPMENT

David Kahn & Donna Breed

With a Foreword by Lanford Wilson

SOUTHERN ILLINOIS UNIVERSITY PRESS

Carbondale and Edwardsville

Designed by Chiquita Babb
Production supervised by Natalia Nadraga
98 97 96 95 4 3 2 1

Library of Congress Cataloging-in-Publication Data
Kahn, David, date.
    Scriptwork : a director's approach to new play
development / David Kahn and Donna Breed ;
with a foreword by Lanford Wilson.
        p. cm.
    Includes bibliographical references and index.
    1. Theater—Production and direction.
    2. Drama—Explication. I. Breed, Donna,
    date. II. Title.
    PN2053.K34 1995
    792'.0233—dc20   94-5425
                                       CIP
        ISBN 0-8093-1985-3
        ISBN 0-8093-1759-1 pbk.

The paper used in this publication meets the minimum requirements of American National Standard
for Information Sciences—Permanence of Paper
for Printed Library Materials, ANSI Z39.48–1984. ∞

CONTENTS

FOREWORD

THIS IS A book about hard work. We who like to say we are involved in the art of the theatre also know we are in the entertainment business. (Like Kenneth Tynan I do not consider entertainment only the act of sitting in the path of a herd of stampeding elephants.) We work hard years to make what we do look effortless. This book tells you how we work.

Stanislavski (an actor before he was a director) formed the Moscow Art Theatre from pragmatism. There were a number of actors in the company with extraordinary talent. He asked them to analyze, probably for the first time, exactly what they did: how they approached a role, what they were experiencing on stage, in rehearsal, in reading a script. He reasoned that the journeyman actor and the tyro could improve if they knew the *process* of acting. From what he learned he devised basic exercises to facilitate the company's work habits. For all the mysticism that surrounds his teaching, really, it was as simple as that—and as difficult.

I don't know why it has taken another hundred years for someone to realize that the art of direction, or understanding how to work on a new play, the *process* of play development, could benefit from the same approach. But I am certainly thankful that someone finally has.

Actors, writers, producers, designers, probably even audiences, can learn as much from this book as the neophyte director, or the bad director, or the good classical director who is working on developing a new play for the first time.

This book may well serve to discourage most would-be directors from working on new plays. It will have made a major contribution to the theatre if it does nothing else.

The process is daunting, but it's necessary, and if there is another book that tells a director how to approach a new script as clearly and correctly as this one does, I don't know of it.

Lanford Wilson

ACKNOWLEDGMENTS

As THIS book goes to press there are some discouraging signs about the health of new script development in the United States. Theatre Communications Group's annual survey of the finances and productivity of the American nonprofit theatre reports a precipitous decline in performance activity for workshops, staged readings, and other developmental activities, with more than 65 percent fewer performances offered in 1993 than 1989—this, despite the "developmental" successes of Tony Kushner's *Angels in America*, Robert Schenkkan's *The Kentucky Cycle*, Susan-Lori Parks's *The America Play*, José Rivera's *Marisol*, and Anna Devere Smith's *Twilight: Los Angeles, 1992*, among others. So, in the face of economic retrenchment that often favors the tried-and-true over the challenge of unknown territory, we acknowledge those theatre artists and institutions that continue to fight the good fight and enjoy the grand adventure of working with playwrights on the creation of new works for the theatre.

Much of the impetus and inspiration for this book comes from the work of those playwrights, directors, and dramaturgs whose interviews grace its second half. Their voices speak to the intelligence, dedication, and good sense that are the essential components of successful collaboration between writers and directors.

There are many others whose work both directly and indirectly informs our approach: Jon Jory and the staff of the Actors Theatre of Louisville show us all how institutional support of new plays can flourish. Lloyd Richards, for many years head of the Yale School of Drama and the National Playwrights Conference, Gordon Davidson and the Mark Taper Forum, South Coast Repertory (whose production of forty-five world premieres in the last fifteen years and other support for new script development has led more than one playwright to refer to the organization as "playwright's heaven"), developmental directors Andre Bishop, Daniel Sullivan, Anne Bogart, Gregory Mosher, Jerry Zaks, Ellen Stewart, John Dillon, Douglas Turner Ward, Carole Rothman, and the productive collaboration between writer Craig Lucas and director Norman René, stand out among the many examples of how and why new script development works.

More directly, this book benefited from its authors' association with institutions centrally involved in the creation of, and support for, new plays. Bay Area Playwrights Festival, The Eureka Theatre Company of San Francisco, New Dramatists, Sierra Repertory Theatre, American College Theatre Festival, Southern Repertory Theatre of New Orleans, San Jose Repertory, and California State University Summer Arts all provided arenas for discovering techniques and working with leading professionals in new script development.

Many individuals gave encouragement, advice, and criticism. Oskar Eustis was our first interview, fresh off his collaboration with writer Emily Mann's *Execution of Justice* and just beginning work on Tony Kushner's *Angels in America*. Oskar's words and sensibilities about the process provided essential kindling for this book and were a guiding light for us as we worked on it. Tom Dunn offered early encouragement and helped us believe we actually had something publishable. David Ball, whose wonderful *Backwards and Forwards: A Technical Manual for Reading Plays* inspired us to submit this manuscript to Southern Illinois University Press, gave us invaluable positive response and raised important concerns that we tried our best to address and that we know made the book stronger. Additional response and helpful suggestions came from Davey Marlin-Jones, Elizabeth Craven, Louise Williams, Marion Kahn,

and especially Lanford Wilson, who wrote a gracious foreword, contributed a terrific interview, and offered invaluable
suggestions on what came in between.

We enjoyed helpful conversations with Tony Taccone, Michelle
Swanson, Catherine Stone, Bill Wollak, and Edward Cohen.
And special thanks are due to our families, our academic
colleagues, and the staff at Southern Illinois University Press
who have borne with us so long on this project.

Finally, my coauthor Donna Breed—whose work on this
book was so often and rudely interrupted by serious illness—
was an example for all who knew and worked with her of
persistence, humor, directness, and acumen. Through these
and so many other qualities Donna Breed embodied the spirit
of collaboration that is the heart of this book.

David Kahn

INTRODUCTION

THERE IS a popular myth about the way new plays are created: a writer labors in isolation for days, weeks, or even years and finally produces a finished script delivered to a producer fully formed and ready for production. In fact, theatre history reveals the inaccuracy of this conception of the playwright working in isolation. Shakespeare did not present his finished scripts to the producer in the historic equivalent of a manila envelope, nor did Molière, Chekhov, Caryl Churchill, or Lanford Wilson. They may have begun work in romantic seclusion, but they completed their scripts and made them great by working on them in the theatre, during rehearsals, until they got them right.

The majority of contemporary American theatre successes begin with development in regional theatres and other workshop venues, where the playwrights benefit from the interaction between their work and the creative contributions of theatre artists and audiences, who help bring the plays to a point of completion. Recent American plays such as *Angels in America, Fences, The Heidi Chronicles, The Grapes of Wrath, Buried Child, Prelude to a Kiss,* and *A Walk in the Woods* did not just appear one day on a commercial producer's desk. They went through extensive processes of development in regional theatres and later moved to Broadway, Off-Broadway, and other commercial and regional theatre venues.[1]

---

1. *Angels in America (Millennium Approaches)*, by Tony Kushner, at Mark Taper Forum and Eureka Theatre Company of San Francisco; *Fences*, by

Many theatre people are getting the message that new plays are not born but made. New play festivals proliferate, colleges sponsor playwrights in residence and premieres of new works, and regional theatres are serving as breeding and testing grounds for the development of original plays—and not only those destined for national commercial recognition, but also new plays made for regional, local, or institutional audiences. According to developmental director Oskar Eustis of Trinity Repertory Company, all this new script work benefits the American theatrical scene because it helps generate the critical mass of activity necessary to produce extraordinary dramatic art:

> Every great writer, every great individual theatre artist, comes at the crest of a wave of healthy theatrical activity. There are waves, and if you don't produce the raw material to make those waves, if you don't have that culture, you're not going to produce the great people who provide paradigmatic signs for what the art form is capable of. You can't just nurture the top. It's not how art forms work.[2]

Within the process of new script development, it is often the director who is the playwright's major collaborator, facilitating the exploratory work of other theatre artists and looking at how a script works as performance. Ideally, the purpose of this collaboration is neither to assess the commercial value of a play nor to secure backers, but rather to provide an environment that enables the playwright to create the most effective script possible, using the laboratory of the theatre to refine the quality of a script in progress. Such research and development can take many forms, each of which gives the

---

August Wilson, at Yale Repertory Theatre; *The Heidi Chronicles*, Wendy Wasserstein, Seattle Repertory Theatre (in association with Playwrights Horizons); *The Grapes of Wrath*, Frank Galati, Steppenwolf Theatre Company; *Buried Child*, Sam Shepard, The Magic Theatre; *Prelude to a Kiss*, Craig Lucas, South Coast Repertory; *A Walk in the Woods*, Lee Blessing, La Jolla Playhouse.

2. Oskar Eustis, Artistic Director, Trinity Repertory Theatre (*see the Appendix*).

playwright and others different kinds of information about how the script works theatrically and what, if anything, needs to be done to ready it for future production.

The director's role in new script development differs from the idea, widely taught in theatre schools, that the director's primary responsibility is to formulate a "concept" and stage it. This "auteur" director marshals all production elements, including the text, to the realization of her vision.[3] The developmental director, on the other hand, does not have that freedom, but must serve the text—and by extension the playwright—by working to *reveal* the script, not use it as an element of directorial virtuosity. The "developmental" director follows the tradition of Harley Granville-Barker, the great elucidator, not Peter Sellars, the great conceptualizer.

Most developmental directors, when asked, maintain that they formulated their approaches to working on new scripts independently and that there is no such thing as a system. However, our own work in new script development and our research into others' practices revealed that there is, in fact, a set of principles and methods widely used though not yet codified.

Scriptwork synthesizes these principles and methods into an approach for working on new plays; it establishes a theoretical framework, defines a set of working terms around which discussion and development can center, and suggests procedures for directing new scripts developmentally and helpfully.

Chapter 1 discusses how to choose projects, where to find new scripts, how to define the working relationship between the playwright and the director, and how to approach legal aspects of new script development.

Chapter 2 delineates the approach for exploring and de-

---

3. In order to achieve a balanced, bias-free style, throughout this book we refer to all directors using the feminine pronoun and all playwrights using the masculine. All actors, regardless of gender, we refer to as actors, not actresses and actors.

veloping the script within the laboratory of the theatre. It specifies the particular responsibilities of actors, designers, and other collaborators when working on new material. It also suggests procedures for casting, incorporating rewrites, and script handling.

Chapter 3 covers the analytical or dramaturgical work that takes place between the director and playwright. It presents a detailed system for analyzing the new script theatrically and for working with the playwright to discover what the script is about and how its elements interact to create the overall theatrical effect.

Chapters 4 and 5 describe the unrehearsed reading, staged reading, developmental workshop, and other exploratory techniques involving the playwright, actors, and other collaborators, including how and when to use audience response and how to decide what kinds of developmental processes, if any, will best serve the script prior to full production.

The Appendix contains extended interviews with developmental directors, dramaturgs, and playwrights. Along with Oskar Eustis, we talked with Marshall Mason of the Circle Repertory Company, Ann Cattaneo, dramaturg at Lincoln Center, Robert Hedley of Temple University, who also ran the Playwrights Workshop at University of Iowa, Morgan Jenness, director of play development at the New York Public Theatre, Alma Becker, developmental director and NEA Fellow, Jack O'Brien, artistic director of San Diego's Old Globe Theatre, and playwrights Lanford Wilson, Phil Bosakowski, Lee Blessing, and Romulus Linney. Their statements provide a real-world perspective on the approaches presented here, revealing some of the controversies in this field and what binds together the practices of new script development.

The techniques presented in *Scriptwork* are a codification of various principles of new script development. The material is presented linearly, though the process is hardly a linear one. Read the techniques as points of departure rather than as a set of instructions and adapt them to each specific situation. Use what you can, reject what you will, and work to establish the things that you find useful to help nurture the play and the writer with whom you are working. The script itself will largely determine the way you work, making its own particular demands on what approaches will best serve the material.

Beware the most significant of several pitfalls in new script work: forcing the play to meet the expectations of the developmental process rather than letting the script and writer determine the nature of support. Playwright Douglas Anderson sounded an important warning in his 1988 discussion of the state of new script development: "New play mechanisms can begin to dictate product. Once a company settles into a particular way of working, it runs the risk of imposing comfortable strategies on recalcitrant material. It can quickly begin to confuse the needs of a text with the voracious demands of text-eating programs."[4]

Along with the script, each artist and each developmental situation creates its own set of requirements. Accommodate the system to the playwright, to your own directorial personality, and to the nature of the director/playwright relationship. If your strength is in script analysis, for example, then your emphasis may be on dramaturgy. If you excel in discovery work with the actors, then you may want to involve them early and use them to do the work in the rehearsal hall that your more solitary counterpart would do with a script and pencil. The playwright may want to talk about the script or might prefer to gauge the results of your work in rehearsals without saying much. He may want actors to do additional research and bring information to rehearsals through improvisation. The script may benefit from a tightening of its logic or from a freeing up of its logic. The key is to select approaches that help reveal and develop the play on its own terms.

In every developmental situation the director and the play-

---

4. Douglas Anderson, "The Dream Machine: Thirty Years of New Play Development in America," *The Drama Review* 32:3 (Fall 1988): 55–84.

wright have a special and unique connection. Many developmental directors describe their working relationships with the playwrights as friendships. This kind of collaborative creative endeavor certainly involves close communication and a personal understanding of each other as well as the script. It is necessary to learn how you and the playwright work best together: maybe it is over coffee at the local diner, or with scripts in hand at the theatre, working intensely into the late hours clarifying a single point, or in round-table discussions with the actors, or in whispered conversations in the back row during rehearsals.

No matter how you personalize these techniques, the important thing to remember is that the heart of this approach is the idea of empowering the playwright and kindling the sparks of a script into a flame by testing and exploring the play in a theatrical context.

Part of our research for this book involved talking with directors, dramaturgs, and playwrights active in new script development. In one of our conversations, developmental director Oskar Eustis, then involved in the early stages of work on Tony Kushner's *Angels in America,* suggested reasons why so much attention is given to new script development these days:

> I think there's actually a fairly simple reason for it: there's a kind of theatre developing in this country that has never existed before.
>
> Until a nonprofit professional theatre existed there was no such thing as a professional noncommercial playwright. When you had commercial playwrights, you had commercial producers. You had an entirely different set of institutional requirements or structures that a play had to go through to get produced. And certainly you had play development work at that time. But, in general, playwrights had to do it by themselves. And if they didn't do it by themselves, they were not produced commercially and they left playwriting. That was all there was

to it. If they could do it by themselves, great, they became successful, serious playwrights. And there weren't very many of them.

Now, there's a kind of theatre responding to the increasing sophistication of audiences, the increasing decentralization of the American theatre, the increasing strength of the regional and nonprofit theatre system. This has created a different breed of playwrights and a different demand for American plays. It's now taken for granted that nonprofit theatres are going to exist in the regions of this country [and] people are starting to say, "What's an American theatrical tradition?" I think, fortunately for all of us, it's begun to be located more and more in the young American playwrights who are coming up.

It's a fundamental shift in how the theatre in this country is structured. Nobody says it's a permanent shift. I happen to think it's a healthy one, but we don't have very deep roots yet. What I do know is that we have the most broad-based, varied, and exciting playwriting going on in America that we've ever had in America's history. That is a result of this system.

Are these people going to stay in the theatre? It depends on what kind of home we provide them. If we provide them a good home, they will.[5]

The best ways to provide good homes for playwrights are to produce their finished plays and offer them consistent support for the development of new ones. In this context skillful developmental directors approach new scripts with respect for the playwright's vision and intentions, using techniques modified to fit each specific constellation of writer, script, and working situation. The methods outlined in this book provide a starting point for developmental directors to collaborate with writers to give them not just a home in the theatre, but a working place.

---

5. Eustis interview.

SCRIPTWORK

1 · CHOOSING

PROJECTS

ACCORDING TO developmental director Davey Marlin-Jones, the first rule of directing new material is, "At the time you are directing, you have to believe that working on this script is the most important thing you could be doing with your life."[1] He calls this kind of commitment to the material the "forty-eight times six question": Are you willing to spend forty-eight hours a week for six weeks in strenuous labor to hear these words and see these actions?

Deciding to work on a play development project involves several crucial decisions: the director's affirmative answer to the "forty-eight times six" question; the playwright's agreement that the script needs development and that this particular director's work will enhance the play; and a mutual definition of an appropriate collaborative process.

Although the director's participation in new script development can occur at many stages of the script writing process, even preceding the playwright's involvement in some cases, this book concentrates on new play development in which the

---

1. "New Play Workshop." American College Theatre Festival, Region VIII, Sonoma State University, Rohnert Park, California, Feb. 13, 1991.

playwright provides at least the first draft of a script. The goal of playwright, director, and actors is to take the script through a developmental situation and emerge with a carefully examined and theatrically tested script.

WHERE TO FIND NEW SCRIPTS

It is not difficult to find unproduced scripts. Usually all you have to do is let it be known that you are looking and scripts will come flooding in. The trick is to find a script that you believe is worth working on.

Generally, the main methods of getting scripts are by solicitation through ads or notices in theatre publications, by conducting a playwriting contest, by talking to people who run playwrights' programs and organizations, through personal acquaintance, and by investigating the finalists in major playwriting competitions. The *Dramatists Sourcebook*, published by Theatre Communications Group, is an excellent resource for further information on acquiring scripts.

DECIDING ON A SCRIPT

Is the Script Worth the Work?

When you first pick up a script under consideration, read it through once very quickly, with the goal of answering one main question: Is this a theatrical, stageable script that is interesting enough to you to make it worthwhile to go through all the sweat and strain involved in the developmental process?

Do not take on a poor script, especially from a writer with whom you have not worked or who is not equipped to fulfill the playwright's responsibilities in the developmental process (see chapter 2). Unless you are convinced that the play and/or the playwright has potential, your work as a developmental director will be intrusive rather than helpful.

Even if you like the material, you may discover that the playwright has not written a theatrical piece at all. The script may actually be a short story, an essay, a sermon, or a poem. If so, your best course is to explore the writer's reasons for choosing the dramatic form and suggest either a more appropriate form or that the writer make the material more dramatic. Writers often resist these kinds of suggestions.

Access

If your answer is yes, the script is worth working on, the second question to ask is: Do I have access to the material? Having access means that you respond to the script somehow, perhaps in terms of the story, a character, a compelling set of images, the issues that it addresses, or the playwright's distinctive voice. Some material will be repugnant to you, some merely uninteresting. Sometimes you will like some things in the script very much, like the world of the play, or the language, or one wonderful scene, but have problems with one or two characters, or how the story develops, or how the events unfold. You probably will not love everything about any script at first encounter, but if you do not connect with the script in some way, you should not work on it.

Need for Development

The next thing to determine is whether your directorial work on the script will make it better. Does the script need some kind of development or is it ready for full production? Playwrights talk about scripts being "developed to death," either subjected to a purgatory of endless readings with no specific goal in mind and no genuine movement toward production, or a series of workshops that seek alterations in the script simply for the sake of "development," unnecessarily tinkering with a play that does not need it or does not benefit from it. Playwrights are understandably wary of these situations and may be reassured by a director's clear statement that the purpose of new script development is to give the writer the opportunity to work on the script on his terms and not subject to the bullying of overzealous dramaturgs or others trying to interfere with the writer's ownership of the material.

Are there specific avenues of exploration that you believe will strengthen the play? What kinds of resources can you bring to bear on the script, both in terms of your own talents and skills and the kinds of developmental processes that you can provide for the playwright?

Now is the time to examine your own motives for choosing this material. What is it that you hope to achieve by working with this script? Do you hope to ride it to a full production someplace? Do you want to ally yourself collaboratively with this particular writer? Do you see yourself as the script's savior? Are you sure that you are responding to what the playwright has written and not to the kind of play that you could turn this into? You need to examine your own agenda with this material, because the playwright is entitled to know how your needs will affect your work on the script.

Playwright's Agreement

Like the director, the playwright chooses to enter a developmental situation. Often the motivation is complex. Playwrights interested in getting their plays produced will frequently seek out organizations and individuals interested in developing new work, seeking whatever activities can be generated around their script, whether a response by a literary manager, a cold reading by a group of actors, or an invitation to produce the script on a company's next season.

Increasingly, the developmental process is considered the route to a full production of a new script and the only way to get the play done or noticed by people who may subsequently produce it. Many playwrights regard this use of "new script development" as a necessary—or unnecessary—evil. The new play reading or developmental workshop is often used as a low-cost market test, the contemporary equivalent of opening out of town. Playwrights are vulnerable to abuse in the name of new play development because they are eager for any response to their work and because the scarcity of production opportunities dictates accommodation to those individuals and institutions who control the theatrical market.

Given this situation, playwrights need to find developmental avenues that help them rather than abuse them. So, like the director, the playwright must examine his motives in entering a collaboration. Does the writer think that the script will genuinely benefit from work with this director and her resources, or is the writer entering the process only because it is a necessary prerequisite to production?

Playwrights who believe in the intrinsic worth of new script development use it as a tool for the exploration and improvement of their scripts. These playwrights seek productive collaborations and hold on to them eagerly once they are established. As Jack Heifner, the author of *Vanities*, says, "I'm always looking for my director, the one who is going to do all my work for the rest of my life."

PRELIMINARY CONVERSATION

If you do not know the playwright whose script you are considering, it is essential to have a conversation before you agree to collaborate. You both need to find out whether you can work together on this project, to discuss each of your motives in seeking a developmental process, and to explore the kinds of work you might do together on the play.

The playwright needs to know whether you read the same play he wrote, whether you can be an advocate of the play, communicating its meaning to other collaborators, and whether you can tell him something illuminating about the play. The playwright also needs to investigate whether you have sufficient dramaturgical and directing skills to undertake this project, what resources you have to offer, and how you envision working on the play together.

The director must do a lot of talking in this first meeting. Remember, you have the benefit of knowing a great deal about how the writer thinks from reading the play; now the writer needs a chance to read you, to learn how you think, how you operate, and what you have to offer. Tell him what you like about the script and what you have questions about. Suggest how you might work on it. Then you can ask the playwright a series of questions regarding his reasons for writing the script, what he wants the script to be, how far along he thinks it is, and what he thinks you might be able to do to help him. Listen carefully to the answers. Make notes of what you say and what he says.

Asking these questions of each other is an excellent way of finding out whether you and the playwright can work together usefully. Listen to what the playwright says and very carefully to how he says it. Now is the time to bail out if you and the playwright have a major disjunction in vocabulary, skill level, or interest in the project or if the playwright is not accessible to you and your approach. Remember, it is much better to withdraw from the association earlier than later. Usually the best thing to do in this case is to thank the playwright for his time, then return the script with a letter saying that you enjoyed reading the piece but upon consideration you do not think that your working on it would be helpful. Wish the playwright every luck with the script, and retire with your dignity, your integrity, and your temper intact.

Legal Issues

It is nearly impossible to construct a standard agreement concerning a director's role in new script development, partly because it is so difficult to define precisely what a developmental director does.[2] Each collaboration establishes its own balance of the director's and writer's contributions, and it is impractical to assign percentages of developmental responsibility since so much of the work is mutual

This can be a highly contentious area of director/playwright collaboration as it involves legal, organizational, artistic, and personal aspects of your work together. It is best to make it absolutely clear that the playwright is responsible for the script, and any authorial claims rest solely with the writer. Directors must realize that the benefits of a collaborative developmental project reside as much in the director's increased experience as in any tangible improvements to the script. Ideally, the playwright and director agree on the terms of the specific developmental project at hand, with no obligations extending beyond this particular phase of your collaboration.

Beyond that, it may be important to discuss the question of formal agreements at the beginning of the process. Determine at what point, if any, a specific contract makes sense and what items it should cover. Try to anticipate situations before they arise. Some of the issues you may consider include compensation; specific acknowledgment of developmental work in subsequent productions or publication of the script; right of first refusal on directing future productions (this may include a buy-out clause providing compensation for the original director); and length of scope of each party's commitment to the project.

Beware agreements that are not reciprocal. For example, is

2. The Society of State Directors and Choreographers (SSD&C) has a contract for when a show is moved to a different venue and a mechanism through which a director may make a grievance against a second director who appropriates the original work without compensation. The SSD&C also has a staff lawyer who is available for consultation on contract matters. The Dramatists Guild flagship contract, the Broadway APC, states clearly that no one should receive payment for a contribution to a script unless he or she has made an "authorial contribution." For clarification of the Dramatists Guild Position on director/dramatist agreements for new script development see Richard Garmise's helpful article "Directors at the Gates," *Dramatists Guild Newsletter* 18:3 (Nov. 1993).

it fair for a director to demand some percentage of income from subsequent productions of a script without agreeing in turn to pay the writer future income derived from directing that script? Directors should never insist, nor playwrights agree, on legal or financial arrangements that inhibit the future prospects of the play such as, for example, a right to direct subsequent productions that prevents the play from being done because a producer is interested in the script but unwilling or unable to hire the director.

Peer issues often determine who can ask what of whom. An influential director's work on a project may create production opportunities for a new playwright; that is a different situation from an established playwright giving an unknown director the chance to participate in a high-profile project.

Another difficulty is that the relationship between director and writer is built on trust, friendship, sympathy, and affinity, all of which make cold, hard, objective business considerations awkward. Developmental director Anthony Taccone of Berkeley Repertory Theatre says the relationship between writer and director is "very much like a marriage," where formal agreements concerning an uncertain future may feel like the distasteful requirement of a prenuptial contract. "Above all," says Taccone, "negotiate something you feel good about that reflects a satisfactory sense of the work and your relationship. The most important thing is to maintain the working relationship you have with the playwright, and set up some kind of structure that allows for changes and reflects the ethical value systems of the individuals involved."[3]

If an institution is involved, there may be requirements and protections imposed by that theatre, such as negotiating a percentage of the writer's royalties on all future productions (5 percent is common) and securing subsidiary rights. For many years, Lloyd Richards, artistic director of the National Playwrights Conference at the Eugene O'Neill Theatre Center,

---

3. Phone interview, April 10, 1993.

insisted on holding an option on all material showcased at the O'Neill until six weeks after the conference closed. This was designed in large part to protect young playwrights from the hoards of overzealous producers who are looking to immediately option (often unfinished) material from the O'Neill immediately following a successful reading. Richards felt that a little breathing space was in the best interest of writers who might want to consider several options including, of course, one from Richards himself.

Individuals involved in new script work should be careful and clear in negotiating the terms of their commitments. There are professional associations for playwrights (The Dramatists Guild) and directors (Society of Stage Directors and Choreographers) seeking guidance in the various legal and contractual aspects of new script development and production.

Working in the developmental process requires a high degree of commitment from all concerned. Thus it is extremely important that you find a script that you can advocate and work for wholeheartedly and a playwright with whom you can establish open and active communication and who trusts you. Once you have done so, you can begin to work developmentally.

2 · DEVELOPMENTAL
APPROACH

A SUCCESSFUL developmental process uses the creative and collaborative forces of the theatre to explore a script and help the playwright refine it—revealing how the play works and does not work as the basis for performance, examining its characters as stage presences, and assessing what theatrical experience the script creates for an audience. The process should serve the positive development of the script, with the playwright's satisfaction and your sense of progressive discovery as the guideposts for the work.

Everyone working with the playwright developmentally—director, actors, and other collaborators—should adopt an approach to the material that is analytical, simple, flexible, openminded, and transparent.

ANALYTICAL

In developmental work, analysis of the script operates in an exploratory rather than a prescriptive manner. This is a time for the playwright and director to develop a common understanding and agreement about the nature of this particular beast by asking and investigating questions raised by the play and their work on it. An analytical approach requires a predisposition for looking closely at the work, a vocabulary for usefully discussing it, time to reflect and respond to the consequences of your discoveries, and the ability to apply the heady work of analysis to the practical development of the script. Analysis is constantly modified as the script develops; acting, directing, and writing choices based on old analyses must be reexamined, and discarded or changed if your exploratory work reveals them as no longer relevant, or strong, or interesting enough.

SIMPLE

At first, work simply, using large directorial and acting strokes, reducing scenes, actions, and characters to their essential components. Look for the framework of action and character; do not try to create a complete performance. You are simplifying deliberately, as a tool to discover the essential structure of the play and its elements. If that essential structure is missing, it is important for the playwright to see that. Clear out the ornamentation so you can see the spine of the play. This is particularly important in short-term developmental work, when all you really have time to do is test the overall shape of the piece and its effect. The developmental process is a reconnaissance, mapping and clarifying the journey that will come with full production. Later, more leisurely rehearsal periods will contemplate the script's complexity.

FLEXIBLE

The nature and excitement of the developmental process are that you can work act 2 on Friday and, as a result of your work, the playwright may have a whole new act 2 on Monday.

Throwing away what you have done and substituting new material can be very difficult for all concerned. It is, however, a necessary condition for developmental work. Remember that the entire purpose of the project is to develop the script that the playwright wants to write, and any movement in that direction is progress. You may decide to suspend work for a time while the playwright goes off and rewrites; you may decide to bring in a different group of actors; you may decide that you need a choreographer on the project; or you may decide that at this particular stage a reading in scuba gear is necessary. The point of the work is to explore the material and to accommodate new discoveries as they arise. Remember also that the previous work is not really gone; the new material is based upon what has gone before.

OPEN-MINDED

There is sometimes the temptation when you are working developmentally to try to make the script conform to a model, either of a specific play or of a genre. If the playwright has come up with a script that reminds you of *Agnes of God*, be sure that you are approaching the script on its own terms and not trying to make it conform to the *Agnes* model. If the script has certain qualities that make it seem to belong to a specific genre, like courtroom drama or farce, be careful that your suggestions are not aimed at making it conform to its genre at the expense of its individuality.

Part of staying open-minded is knowing your own biases so that you can allow for the ways they influence your responses. There is nothing wrong with having biases, and you will doubtless choose scripts and playwrights whose writing falls within your preferential territory; just know what they are so that you can be aware of any pressure to insert them into the playwright's writing. For example, you may have a penchant for long scenes and thus guide the playwright to collapse two scenes into one when the script really should be a series of short scenes. You may like lots of character information in the form of monologues and exposition, when the playwright is purposely trying to keep character motives mysterious. You may like boffo first-act curtains and ask for one when it is inappropriate to the patterns of the script. Make sure that you continue to focus on the playwright's play, not yours. If there is a mismatch between the playwright's intention and your biases, work for the intention.

TRANSPARENT

Developmental directing is different from other directing in that your work as a director must aim at transparency; you want the *play* to be visible, not what you have overlaid directorially. The two most important ways to remain transparent are (1) refrain from applying a concept to the script that is not inherent in the playwright's words, and (2) resist the temptation to use all your director's tricks and techniques to make it work.

Do Not Hide the Play with Your Concept

Directors are trained to place a concept on a script; most directing textbooks start with that chapter. Being transparent requires that you do not conceptualize the script heavily, because it is not finished and any imposition of a conceptual structure may force the script to go in the direction of the director's vision, not the playwright's. Generally it is best to leave the concept to directors who come after you or for your second production of the material. Understand, however, the difference between opacity and legitimate directorial responses that illuminate the text and sometimes clarify it for the playwright. For example, shifting a play's period from post-nuclear-holocaust New York City to fourteenth-century

France is probably not an appropriate choice for a developmental director, whereas using human actors to play the horses in *Equus* probably is.

Do Not Try to Fix Things Directorially

In most directing, the director's job is to *make* the script work; in developmental directing, your job is to see *whether* the script works. Sometimes it is extremely useful for the playwright to see a script up on its feet, even in front of an audience, to understand that a particular scene or character does not work as intended. To this end, you must be careful to let scenes and characters stand on their own.

If you and the playwright agree that a scene or a moment is not working you may suggest directorial tactics that you can use. Sometimes, for example, it is possible to provide an extra-textual effect, like a sunset, an explosion, a projected image, or a dumb-show, that will make the playwright's point when the script fails to do so. Inform the playwright, "To get between points A and C, I could insert the exploding volcano effect. Does that fall within your intentions for this script?" If the playwright agrees with your suggestion he may wish to include it in future versions of the text.

Whether you show the playwright the problem or you fix it directorially, the point of transparency is to reveal what is in the script and what is not and to allow the playwright to decide what to do about it.

AREAS OF RESPONSIBILITY

The developmental process works best when responsibilities within the process are clearly assigned and differentiated so that all concerned can get on with their own jobs. Confusion, muddle, inefficiency, and ill feelings often follow closely upon the overstepping of lines of responsibility.

Therefore, it is important early in the process to specify the responsibilities of the participants. Playwrights write, directors direct, actors act, and so on. Each collaborator approaches work on the script with a particular purpose and a specific language dictated by the area of responsibility. An actor, for example, should work on the script as an actor, using actor's language, and avoid the tendency to get into issues of playwriting and directing. As the process gets going, these lines tend to blur somewhat; in some cases the playwright may ask the director and actors to participate in some of the writing. That is fine, as long as all concerned understand who has the primary responsibility for each area; that way you can go back to the original assignments if lines of responsibilities get too confused.

What the Playwright Does

The playwright provides the script that is the center of the process, decides what is to be done to the script and, during the process, has the final say on what stays in the script and what goes. All the participants in the developmental process are working to realize the playwright's vision. It is up to the playwright to answer the questions that the developmental process raises or to leave them as questions. It is the playwright's script.

Specific Tasks. During the developmental process, the playwright is responsible for:

- providing the script that will be developed;
- participating openly in the developmental process. That is, being willing to take the discoveries of the process and implement them in terms of his own particular working methods, writing style, and vision;
- writing, rewriting, and cutting, either on his own or after consultation with the developmental director, based on the

information and discoveries of the director, actors, and other collaborators;
- attending rehearsals regularly and working from observation and discussions about rehearsals with the developmental director;
- acknowledging the work of this company in subsequent productions or publications.

What the Director Does

The developmental director's primary responsibility is to use the process to facilitate the theatrical exploration of the script, working with the playwright to undertake unpressured exploration of the material, critically examining what is being revealed, and communicating ongoing responses to the playwright.

Specific Tasks. Most traditional director's tools—like scheduling, organizing, script analysis, staging, guiding actors, shaping dynamics, rhythm, and tempo, and keeping an overall eye on the process—will be useful to the developmental director; the main differences lie in the approach to the material and goals for the process, discussed above.

In the developmental process, the director is responsible for:

- choosing the script;
- analyzing the script dramaturgically;
- with the playwright, specifying the kind of developmental process;
- scheduling rehearsals and public presentations;
- casting actors, in consultation with the writer, and guiding their work;
- keeping participants working within their appropriate areas;
- running rehearsals according to the kind of developmental process selected;
- performing ongoing analyses as the script changes;
- working with the playwright in and away from rehearsal;
- receiving, collating, and interpreting response to the work;

- working with other personnel (designer, choreographer, composer, etc.) before and during the process;
- meeting with the playwright afterward to summarize, reflect, and decide on next steps.

What the Actor Does

In the developmental process, the actor functions in two ways simultaneously, (1) as a test subject, so the playwright and developmental director can look at the material on its feet, and (2) as a full collaborator who discovers and establishes the basic perimeters and core of the character. By working on the characters and by reporting on their work, actors reveal things about the characters and the entire script that cannot be discovered any other way.

Specific Tasks. The developmental actor uses all the traditional acting tools—finding and playing the character's intentions, obstacles, tactics, discoveries, and major transitions—within the simple, flexible, open-minded, and analytical guidelines discussed above.

In the developmental process, the actor is primarily responsible for:

- discovering the character's journey through the play;
- determining whether the character's actions and responses make sense;
- establishing the character's relationships with others in the play;
- seeing if the playwright provides enough clues to develop a character;
- testing the character for performability, plausibility, interest, and lack of banality;
- providing ideas for character development based on the rehearsal investigations;
- being open and available for changes in the text.

Techniques of Developmental Acting. Begin with simple, clear, singular approaches to the various sections of the material.

Find and play strong intentions, obstacles, and tactics, but simplify them as much as possible. For each scene, give the character one primary motivation, find the essential conflict, and choose a clear emotional response to the given situation. Actors will add character elaboration and complexity in the next stage of the process, after the basics are established. Keep asking simple questions: What is the character's function in the play? What does the character want? What stands in her way? What does she do to get what she wants? Make sure that the character's actions, responses, emotions, and characteristics are consistent with the world in which the character lives—the world of the play.

Actors then need to link the character's actions, focusing on what, if anything, connects the events causally, so that A leads to B leads to C, taking careful note of where the connections and transitions are obvious, where they have to work to find them, and where they cannot find them.

Actors try to derive a playable character from the clues in the script and make sure that when they go outside the script they make that known. They need to discover whether the playwright has provided enough material for them to create the characters. As with the developmental director, actors should avoid trying to fix the character or to cover up weaknesses in the script. The developmental task is to see *whether* and *how* the character functions and to let the playwright see what works and what does not. Be particularly careful not to turn to a performer's bag of tricks to make the character work. That is, do not play with voices or character twitches, limps, or tics unless the script specifically requires such behavior or unless the playwright and director know these devices are employed and why.

If actors have to do something outrageous or take extreme extratextual measures to make a scene or a transition work, the director and writer need to know about it. For instance, it is extremely useful if the actor can say, "I had to go crazy after so-and-so left, even though it isn't in the script, because otherwise there was no way to get the character overwrought enough to commit suicide. Does that work with what the playwright wants?"

Above all, actors must remain flexible. Rewrites may come in frequently. Sometimes they are major. Developmental actors are particularly careful not to get too attached to the character as it develops and must be able to put aside previous work and incorporate the new at a moment's notice, not confining a developing character within predetermined boundaries. Sometimes rewrites require significant changes in acting choices already made. In fact, actors must even be willing to abandon the character if it proves unnecessary to the script, or to have a character redefined in such a way that it needs to be recast with another actor.

OTHER CONTRIBUTORS TO THE DEVELOPMENTAL PROCESS

The script development process can benefit from the contributions of other theatrical collaborators, such as dramaturg, designers, and producer.

Dramaturg

This book assumes that there is no dramaturg assigned to the process, but rather that the developmental director functions as a dramaturg on the material. If the project does have a dramaturg, then the director's tasks can be divided and more things can be accomplished. The dramaturg assists with research and analysis.

Research. If the play is based on factual or historical realities, the dramaturg can research the actual events, characters, place, period, or issues and provide, in various forms, the results of the research. A dramaturg may assist in checking points of historical accuracy, adding information, or pointing out discontinuities. As with the director, the dramaturg must work strongly from the play's intention, contributing that which might strengthen the playwright's work and not simply distracting him with gratuitous trivia.

Analysis. The dramaturg may act as a sounding board for the director's analysis, pointing out patterns, issues, images, character functions, and other elements that contribute to the play's meaning. Dramaturgs should be skilled in the mechanics of dramatic structure and can be helpful in identifying how the play is constructed and what models might be useful for analysis. Dramaturgs are generally knowledgeable about the processes of playwriting and can respond specifically and technically to the ways that both the writer and the writing operate. Playwright Douglas Anderson once offered a good description of an ideal dramaturg as one who "would combine theoretical brilliance, encyclopedic knowledge of dramatic literature, performance smarts, and super interpersonal skills. And a little clairvoyance would come in handy."[1]

Above all, the dramaturg's work is investigative and not prescriptive. As Romulus Linney once said, "Dramaturgs have three great instinctive urges: to eat, have sex, and rewrite someone else's play." Terrence McNally put it more directly: "I think a dramaturg can do more harm than good. . . . I have seen plays so rewritten and improved at the behest of a well-intentioned dramaturg that the actual life force that caused them is stifled."[2] Consequently, developmental directors should use dramaturgs who advocate the play based on its own qualities rather than on a preconception of what the play, or a play, should be. Also, dramaturgs should always work in

---

1. Douglas Anderson, "The Dream Machine: Thirty Years of New Play Development in America," *The Drama Review* 32:3 (Fall 1988): 79.
2. Terrence McNally, "How a Playwright Guards His Vision," *New York Times*, 7 Dec. 1986, sec. 2, p. 1.

concert with the developmental director. Mutual trust and a consistency of signals are essential as more collaborators start responding to the script.

Designers

How a play works is often very closely tied to the technical methods of its presentation. A designer's perspective gives form to the world of the play and establishes the physical context for the script's events in performance. Designers read plays with their own set of priorities and can make discoveries, reveal problems, and offer insights that may elude playwrights, actors, and directors. Sometimes a designer provides a key to the play, as Jo Mielziner did for *Death of a Salesman* by creating an environment that unified the various temporal and spatial elements of the play. Mielziner's see-through house provided a powerful metaphor for the play, already suggested by its original title, *The Inside of His Head*. Mielziner's set allowed Willie Loman's memories and delusions to flow more freely into the narrative events of the story. The revelation of this design approach significantly altered Miller's organization of the play and served to strengthen its intention.

In most developmental processes the various designs will not be concretely realized. However, the designer's vision of the physical world of the play, in the form of ideas, images, and even sketches or models can serve to ground the script in a specific theatrical reality for the writer and his collaborators and for audiences who may participate in readings of this script.

Producers

The economic stakes in producing new plays are so high that, increasingly, many producers are involved in all phases of new script development. Producers must be sensitive to the particular needs of the developmental process and not try to rush a script into production or demand unqualified success from every developmental project. The purpose of development is unpressured exploration and the freedom to experiment in an atmosphere where the consequences of the work are solely in the hands of the playwright. Producers in new script development must be advocates for the play and ensure that the process of collaboration is in concert with the writer's impulses.

In this way, a producer's contributions can be of significant benefit, marshaling the resources of the theatre in service of the writer. As Bill Hemming, literary manager for Circle Rep, notes, "Our resident playwrights don't write in isolation. They have a professional theatre with all its resources behind them, and its entire staff ready to support them at any stage of the writing process in which the writer feels he or she needs help: from germinal idea, through first draft, all the way to a fully mounted production."[3]

A good producer for new script development will foster communication between participants and provide the resources necessary for the most effective development of the script with the understanding that not every project will turn into *A Chorus Line*. The ultimate consideration is *not*, Will it sell? That decision and those considerations come later. The questions for the developmental process are, What is it? and What can it become through our work on it? Nurturing many projects in this manner is the best way to create exciting new theatre.

Also, while you do not want to inhibit the playwright's vision with mundane practicalities, the theatre is a business. A producer's perspective can mean the difference between a producible play and a closet drama, and it may be useful to consider the economic realities of the theatre profession and the opportunities for the play's subsequent production from

---

3. Lee Alan Morrow and Frank Pike, *Creating Theatre: The Professionals' Approach to New Plays* (New York: Vintage Books, 1986), 246.

the practical viewpoint of someone who knows the business of producing new scripts. Make sure that, whether you are hiring a producer or working for one, you have a common understanding of what each of you wants from the project.

DEVELOPMENTAL SUPPORT

The addition of even minimal support to the developmental process helps you get more done more efficiently. A script assistant, who handles duplicating and facilitates the distribution of rewrites and keeps close track of what goes on in rehearsals and meetings, is invaluable. You may need to provide a place for the playwright to work. You certainly need adequate copy facilities and budget. You need a place to rehearse, with access to some sort of basic rehearsal furniture. As the working process employs more and more tools of the theatre, increased production support is often required.

CASTING

In developmental work, you must involve the playwright in casting and cast as close as possible to the playwright's ideal. When the playwright participates in casting sessions you will learn things about his view of the characters from discussions about which actors are right or wrong for the roles. Conversely, your ideas about casting may provide the playwright with new insight into the characters and how they might be played.

It is not always possible to cast to the playwright's vision without sacrificing the acting skills necessary for the developmental process. Actors who make clear, text-based choices, and who can play strong intentions—whether psychological or theatrical—are worth more to you than actors who simply look like the playwright's picture of the characters. Over the duration of the developmental process the playwright will likely find that his pre-casting idea of the characters changes to include what the actual actors bring to the roles.

Choose actors who fulfill the requirements discussed in *Areas of Responsibility*. If you do not have access to experienced developmental actors, check your potential actors' working reputations very carefully and avoid any who are rigid, temperamental, or excessively slow. You want flexible, open-minded, creative actors, who can gracefully accommodate frequent script modifications and changing character identity. Remember, the actors are not, at this point, preparing fully sculpted performances but rather exploring foundations for the characters' future development.

REWRITES

Throughout the developmental process, the playwright will probably be cutting, rearranging, and rewriting. The playwright determines what alterations are necessary in several ways, through his own observations of how the play is working or not working in rehearsal and through questions posed by the director or actors.

Often a simple question or statement is enough: "The scene is too long" or "I don't understand why she throws the baby out the window" or "Why does this scene take place in an elevator?" Exploratory writing exercises around questions raised in the developmental process may help the writer address a troublesome area in a new way, by writing freely on material that may never be incorporated in the final script but may unlock a key moment. Sometimes playwrights benefit from actor improvisations around unclear events or issues.

Necessary rewrites can be encouraged by providing time and space for the playwright to work. Be sensitive to the playwright's creative methods. If he needs green ink, an all-night writing session, and a portrait of Eugene O'Neill for inspiration, try to provide them.

Throughout the developmental process, everyone involved should prepare, both conceptually and procedurally, to accommodate revisions. While this process is exciting, it can also be unsettling and strenuous—but the entire purpose of the developmental process is to explore the script and implement whatever changes the playwright desires.

Putting in Rewrites

Putting in rewrites takes several forms: changing a word here and there, changing a line or two in a scene, or deleting or adding entire sections of scripts.

The script assistant or the stage manager maintains the master script and transmits changes to the developmental director and actors. The script assistant meets with the playwright well before rehearsal time, gets the list of minor changes, duplicates the major ones, hole-punches the new pages to fit into the existing scripts, and then, at the very beginning of each rehearsal, conducts the session where the company incorporates rewrites.

These rewrite-insertion sessions can be time-consuming and confusing, but it is absolutely necessary that everyone obtain the same information at the same time and that the script assistant checks carefully to see that everyone understands the changes. Typical directions might be:

- On *page 4*, three lines down, change "Molly, I love you" to "Molly, I wish you wouldn't do that!"
- Remove *page 5* entirely; make a note on the top of *page 6* that there is no longer any *page 5*.
- After *page 6*, insert *page 6A*, and cut the first three speeches on *page 7*.
- In act 2, remove the entire scene between Molly and Liam, (*page 34*), and add this new scene (*pages 34a, 34b,* and *34c,* dated with today's date).

The script assistant must check as she goes along to be sure that everyone understands. Individuals comprehend these instructions at their own speed, so the pace of the rewrite-insertion session must graciously accommodate the slowest member of the company. It does no good at all to get irritated.

It is useful if the actors and director receive a master list of all the changes along with extra pages. New pages should be dated so you can tell easily which version is current. Everyone should fold, spindle, mutilate, or otherwise deface and remove the old pages as soon as the correct changes are in place. Keep only "live" pages in your working scripts. Let the script assistant or the playwright be the archivist of the old versions. Director and actors need to concentrate on the new material and let the old go.

Before you begin the rehearsal, read all the changes out loud to ensure that everyone has the right pages and words and is minimally familiar with the new material.

Note: If you have a public presentation scheduled, some actors may become more resistant to revisions because continuing changes threaten the work they have already done. This is especially true of actors who memorize readily. It is thus important to keep your actors from memorizing and to continue to remind them that they are in a developmental process, not a traditional performance situation, and are not expected or required to create finished, memorized performances.

Script Handling

Actors working in a developmental process need to organize their scripts so that they can insert and remove pages easily. It is extremely important that the actors be able to handle the scripts with one hand and that the pages do not go flying all over in rehearsal. Some sort of cheap three-ring binder is satisfactory. Prong binders are clumsy when you need to change the material frequently. Pages fall off clipboards at inopportune times, and loose pages are absolutely unsatisfactory. Make all markings in scripts in pencil.

NEXT STEPS

In any developmental process there are various things you can do with a script, either singly or in concert, and different orders in which to do them. Sometimes the playwright finds a simple unrehearsed reading with experienced actors more useful than elaborate workshops or analyses; sometimes he may want you to run a complete dramaturgical analysis on the script and convey your findings to him; sometimes the playwright learns what he needs to know by sitting in an audience and listening to their response as the script is performed in a staged reading; sometimes the script will move directly into production. There is no single order of procedure for new script work that is correct or preferable. How you continue depends on what the playwright needs and wants.

The next several chapters discuss the various approaches you can take to a new script. You may choose any or all of them, and you may execute them in whichever order seems most useful to the playwright. Use them as a menu of developmental techniques, not as a prescribed sequence.

3 · DEVELOPMENTAL
DRAMATURGY

To DIRECT a production . . . means administering to the spiritual welfare of the playwright and at the same time taking into account the temporal needs of the theatre; establishing the point of view of one evening and of eternity; handling the text of a play, hand in hand with the author, as if it were a magic formula. Directing is the opposite of criticism: the critics, zigzagging between laws and rules on one side and their own pleasure on the other, navigate in the theatre by trying to sound their reactions with an old fathom-stick in one hand and with the other sighting the play through a pair of old marine-glasses. Directing a play is the exact opposite of this. It means constantly searching for reasons that will explain liking and admiration. It means living according to poets' rules. It means comporting with the gods of the stage, with the mystery of the theatre. It means being honest and straightforward in the art of pleasing. And sometimes, too, it means making mistakes.[1]

In new script development you are solving the mystery of the script for the first time. No matter what specific developmental process you undertake, conducting a paper analysis or

---

1. Louis Jouvet, "The Profession of the Producer, II," *Theatre Arts Monthly* 21 (Jan. 1937): 57–64 (trans. Rosamond Gilder).

developmental dramaturgy is an important step, valuable even if it is the only developmental work you do on a script. You may perform dramaturgical analysis as a preliminary procedure before you go into rehearsals and as a way of determining the course of further developmental work. You will certainly continue to perform, either formally or informally, the kinds of analyses presented here at all stages of the developmental process.

Developmental dramaturgy is theatrical dramaturgy: you study the script with a director's sensibility, understanding it as it will work on the stage and not just as a piece of dramatic literature. This is what one playwright calls "reading the script in three dimensions," envisioning the theatre that it will produce.

The system and sequence offered here are models designed to be adapted to each situation. Your process and vocabulary may differ, but you should find correspondences between your dramaturgical approach and terminology and what is offered here. As with the rest of the material in *Scriptwork*, these methods are broken down and presented linearly. In practice, however, this kind of analysis tends to operate more organically, proceeding from the unique form of the text and personalities of the playwright and director.

It is possible that you may never discuss this analysis with the playwright or use any of this dramaturgical vocabulary with him. Some playwrights respond well to an analytical approach and some prefer that you respond in intuitive, non-linear terms. If the playwright does not want to hear detailed analyses, keep your charts and diagrams to yourself and respond in language that the playwright finds useful. Remember, however, that reliable intuition is based on internalized technique, so the better your analytical work on a script the better and more reliable your intuitions concerning it.

What follows is a sequential and formal dramaturgical analysis designed as a means of providing definitions and suggesting a mechanical process. Without delving too far into the metaphor, we believe that this process is like a guide to love-making—not step-by-step instructions, but a useful list of considerations and techniques.

Everything you do in developmental dramaturgy is aimed at getting you to understand the script in terms of its *intention*—what you believe the script is trying to convey. Only by analyzing the various theatrical devices or *elements* that the playwright uses and their *emphasis*—how they are organized— can you appreciate the *experience* that the play will create for the audience. And it is in the audience's experience that the fulfillment of the play's intention is realized.

The outline of this dramaturgical model looks like this:

- determine the play's *intention*
- examine the script's *elements*:
  —the *world of the play*
  —the *story* and its conventions
  —the play's *issues*
  —the *event chain*
  —the *characters* as they exist functionally, relationally, and individually
  —the *patterns* and how they work
- determine the *emphasis*, or how the playwright has organized the elements
- understand the *experience* that the play will create for the audience

INTENTION

Theatrical analysis begins, proceeds, and ends with contemplation of the play's intentions. A script is a conscious creation of form and function that exists for a reason: to communicate something—its intention—through theatrical elements such as story, events, characters, issues, patterns of images and language, and the distinctive world of the play. The best plays use each element to support and strengthen the communication of the play's intention, and conversely, the play's intention dictates every other theatrical choice.

Intention is a more expansive term than theme, idea, concept, or moral. Intention is *what the play does*, a cumulative result of the play's emotional and intellectual content. It is defined by your interpretation of the meaning that the play creates, produced by everything that the play contains. It is what the play does to you, the reaction—in the chemical sense—that it brings about in an audience. A play's intention is active and may be essentially defined by the following formula: to communicate [something] by [certain means]. The director may say, "The intention of the play, as I see it, is to do this to this audience, and this is how it does it." For example, *The Glass Menagerie* demonstrates the impossibility of escaping the past by showing Tom haunted by memories of his family and by his decision to leave them. He relives the past in an attempt to gain absolution for his desertion and to exorcise his ghosts. The incidents he recounts hold him prisoner. The way his memory encapsulates Laura, Amanda, and Jim emphasizes those qualities about them that continue to obsess him.

It is both difficult and reductive to extract a simple statement of intention from a script. In fact, if it is easy to state the intention, then you probably have a simplistic play. Indeed, a play may have an intention that cannot be summarized in a single statement. More complex plays may involve multiple layers of meaning, where the connections are not immediately obvious. Try to identify what, if anything, ties the play together and how each layer contributes to an overall intention. This kind of multiplicity may suggest that the play is a masterwork, or it may be a sign that the play is disorganized or is trying to do too many things at once.

Determining intention is always a matter of interpretation. That is why there are so many different responses to any given play. What intention you derive from a play depends upon what you bring to it; no two people will find precisely the same intention, although if the play is a good one they will probably find some linkage between their interpretations. In developmental directing, the important thing is to communicate your understanding of the play, to ensure that your interpretation is aligned with the playwright's intention and that it has its basis in what is actually contained in the script.

Your understanding of the play's intention may not match what the playwright thinks he wrote. Often the sum of the play's effects creates a more significant intention than that originally conceived by the writer. Your analysis may open up areas of the play that the playwright had not considered or consciously constructed. Sometimes you cannot discover the intention that the playwright is working for. In either case, respond to the script without prejudice, letting the playwright know what you found in it.

Your understanding of the script's intention will continue to change as you work on the play. The important thing is to keep returning to discussion and analysis of the intention throughout the developmental process, to prompt questions about the play and to guide the choices you make.

ELEMENTS

The *elements* of this system of new script development comprise: world of the play, story, issues, event chain, characters, and patterns. This list of theatrical elements is neither complete nor prioritized. There is no definitive list of theatrical elements nor any formula for how they must be used; the theatrical elements themselves are neither separate nor equal. Each playwright decides which elements to use and how best to employ them. Each script therefore demands its own distinct approach, focusing on how the use of these elements and their emphasis relate to the play's intention.

EMPHASIS

Emphasis is the weight or priority given to the various elements, which will differ from play to play. For example, Beckett's

Waiting for Godot emphasizes circular patterns of character, language, and activities; Pinter's *The Room* emphasizes the claustrophobic world of the play; Blessing's *A Walk in the Woods* highlights character interaction; and Feydeau's *A Flea in Her Ear* emphasizes farcical events inspired by mistaken identity and ludicrous situations resulting from coincidence.

Identifying which element(s) the playwright chooses to emphasize will give you important information. It will tell you where the leading edge of the play is or where the playwright has chosen to place most of his attention. It may also reveal imbalances, where one element is thoroughly explored at the expense of others. The play's issues may be articulated in detail but through characters who have no dimensionality and who arouse no response. When you read the play for emphasis you are looking at how these balances operate. You will be less likely to make *Still Life* into *All My Sons* if you understand that Mann has written a collage of character revelations while Miller has constructed a complex sequence of interdependent events.

Understanding how the script emphasizes its elements often determines where your explorations and discussions will center. If the play emphasizes characters, you will focus on their dimensionality and development. In this case you may bring actors into the process relatively early, to help you bring the characters to life. If the script emphasizes a distinctive world, you will spend a large portion of your time examining how all the pieces of the play reinforce the world and may want to bring in a designer to help you understand the physical environment.

EXPERIENCE

Ultimately, every play creates an *experience* for an audience in the theatre. Each of the play's elements and the way they function together contributes to the audience's perception of how the play moves through time and space and what it all means. This sum of what is communicated to the audience creates the total effect: the play's experience. Ideally, this is the fulfillment of the script's intention, though realistically the audience's response is often much more (or much less) than the creators of the work expect.

For the audience, the experience of the play in performance may be intellectual, emotional, spiritual, and, in the most exciting plays, all of these and more. The experience may center on particular moments in the play and it may involve a cumulative reaction to the play's total impact. It will affect different audiences in different ways. In the best of theatrical worlds, the experience of the play will continue to resound long after the play has ended, moving out of the theatre and into the lives of the audience.

The objective of developmental directing is to discover the experience that the play creates and how the script's individual elements contribute to or detract from that experience. When you first read a script as a director, you make an initial prediction about what experience the script will create. Then you check that prediction in a number of ways: by analyzing it, by having it read by actors, by rehearsing it, and ultimately by how the play actually affects an audience in performance.

DRAMATURGICAL ANALYSIS

A Cautionary Note: Many of the following questions concern consistency, causality, and logical connections, but not all plays are or should be linear or causal. Be sure that you, as a developmental director, understand that it is not your job to force models of playwriting upon the script. Awareness of models is important: recognizing a play's conscious or unconscious debt to dramaturgical precedent may help you identify how a play's structure operates or where deviation raises questions and offers new possibilities. While all your knowledge of dramatic structure, criticism, history, and literature will be valuable, use these resources in a nonrestrictive manner to help understand what is in the play and how it works on its own terms. You must begin to grasp the playwright's style, in the large sense of the kind of play he is trying to write and the way he chooses to present his material. You want to elicit the script's intention and how the playwright organizes and emphasizes the theatrical elements to support that intention. For example, you do not want to force the script into a predetermined linear, logical construct, if that is not what the playwright is trying to do or say. Perhaps the play's intention is to deny logic and linearity. Look at the play and not the genre.

Everything Is Everything. The procedures outlined below are inherently artificial. It is impossible to read a script for only one thing at a time, and you may not analyze the elements in the order presented here. Nevertheless, for the purposes of this discussion and for efficiency in focusing your analytical work, try to concentrate on only one or two elements in the script during each reading, knowing that considerations of the play's issues, for example, cannot really be separated from its images.

Preliminary Reading: The Overview

The preliminary reading is your chance to familiarize yourself with the script as a whole, as a prelude to more detailed analytical work. From this reading you should be able to speculate about the experience that the script creates and how that experience is a fulfillment of the playwright's intention.

Read the script quickly from start to finish. Do not take notes or mark the script. When you finish, notice lightly your general response to the material. Think about the script, but be careful not to make any corrective judgments about it. Jot down a few general notes, focusing on the following kinds of questions: What moves me? What is exciting? What are the strengths of the play? What elements are most emphasized? What happens in the play? Why the title? Are there distinctive characters? Are there definable relationships between them? See if you can make a general statement about the particular ambiance that the play creates and the rules that seem to hold within it.

From these initial responses, derive a preliminary, and necessarily flexible, statement of the playwright's intention. Try to state it in one sentence. Write it down. Be prepared to modify this statement many times as your analytical and theatrical work continues. You may not achieve a satisfactory statement of the script's intention until the project is finished.

Let the script sit for a couple of days and then read it again with pencil in hand.

Reading for the World of the Play, the Story, and the Issues

In this technical reading you begin to anatomize the script, examining how several of the elements operate. Focus your attentions on making a preliminary formulation of the world the script creates and identifying the story and the issues raised. Evaluate these elements in light of how they derive from, support, or change your understanding of the script's intention.

World of the Play. Each play creates its own specific rules that govern its people and events, establishing the logic against which the plausibility of everything in the script is tested. The world of the play is shaped by a combination of both its internal and external logics.

The *internal logic* is defined by the fictive or make-believe world being represented. It is manifested through the story, encompassing the given circumstances, the behavior of the characters, and the environment in which the story is set:

medieval Denmark, for example, threatened from without, a king's ghost haunting the battlements, a queen married to her late husband's brother, her son disgusted by it all and grappling with thoughts of revenge.

This fictive world of the play may bear little or no resemblance to the world as we know it in our lives or have seen it in other plays. Statues may come to life, curses may have inevitability, words may kill, ghosts may torment or seduce the living, the king's messenger may save the day, time may move backwards or sideways or cease to exist, entire crowds may break into song and dance or even become rhinoceroses. Everything is relative to the play's particular portrait of reality and anything may happen and be accepted by an audience within the framework of the play's internal logic.

Another aspect of the world of the play is its *external logic*, which comprises the "rules of engagement" between the play and the audience, or its performance conventions. The play's external logic may include the use of formal conventions of language, such as blank verse or rhymed couplets. The playwright may employ asides and various other direct-address and audience-inclusion conventions, such as the audience as an onstage witness in Shaffer's *Equus* or as a target of attack in Genet's *The Blacks*, or its applause as a magical agent in Barrie's *Peter Pan*. Performance conventions may ask us to accept the use of masks, odd manipulations of time and space, the use of a single gesture to represent a total psychological state, acknowledgment of a lighting instrument as the source of romantic moonlight, the use of three actors to play a single character—in short, any mode of communication operating on the performance level.

Analyzing the world of the play is like exploring an unknown universe. Previously known realities do not necessarily apply. Every scrap of theatrical expression is a clue to the geography, inhabitants, and laws of the place. The logic of a playwright's particular vision of the world as expressed in a given script is a key to understanding how the rest of the play is organized and how it all operates on stage, enabling actors and director to distinguish acceptable and appropriate choices.

Story. The story is the play's narrative thrust. You can analyze a play's story in two ways: literally or essentially. The literal story of the play comprises its narrative details, what actually happens and who does what to whom. The essential story is the central dramatic action that remains when the specific narrative details are eliminated, the generic or archetypal statement of what happens in the play. The literal story of *Oedipus the King*, for example, involves the details of his personal history, present relationships, problems, and how they play themselves out when he attempts to remove the plague from Thebes. The essential story is a man's discovery of the truth about himself. In *The Cherry Orchard*, the literal story is a complex interweaving of the desires and frustrations of the Ranevsky family and their followers played out over the course of many months. The essential story is the family's loss of their old way of life.

The story of a play can be a powerful focus of the play's elements, often serving as the impetus for events, characters, and ideas. Story dictates the play's internal logic. Indeed, the kind of story it is, especially if it conforms to archetypal or generic patterns, often requires that elements be articulated and emphasized in certain ways. For example, Shaffer's *Sleuth*, a mystery story, employs the devices of foreshadowing, hidden information, and surprise reversals. Feydeau's farcical story in *Hotel Paradiso* uses mistaken identity, chance encounters, broad characterizations, and lightning-paced events. The surrealistic story in Strindberg's *Ghost Sonata* uses the symbols, character transformations, and disjointed time frame of the dream state.

In the modern and postmodern theatres, some plays de-emphasize or submerge the narrative story in an attempt to capture another kind of experience: for example, the exploration of issues in Shawn's *Aunt Dan and the Lemon*, the ex-

pression of unconscious patterns of perception in Maeter-
linck's *The Intruder*, and the creation of a ritual in the Living
Theatre's *The Brig*. Historically, however, most plays are articulated around their stories.

Story is one of the easier elements to isolate analytically,
and if you find you are unable to extract the story you may
have an important pointer to the kind of play you are working
on, indicating either a lack of narrative clarity or that the play
is organized around another element.

Issues. A playwright may have specific issues that he wishes
to address, sometimes overtly stated and didactically expressed
as in Brecht's *Lehrstücke*. More often the issues are woven into
the other theatrical elements, creating an interaction between
the intellectual arguments and the life of the play. In Clark's
Whose Life Is It, Anyway? for example, the question of "right
to die" flows through the play and serves as a catalyst for its
events, language, physical images, and character reactions. In
fact, the major pattern in the play is the repeated exploration
of this issue, and all the play's elements stem from the question
posed in the title.

Weiss's *Marat/Sade* abounds with issues examined from multiple perspectives. The central issue of revolution, for example,
is explored through several layers of the play: the "historical" characters confront political and personal aspects of the
French Revolution; the inmates of the asylum engage in their
own revolution against their keepers; references to modern
revolutions are pointedly expressed; and the very qualities of
theatrical performance in *Marat/Sade* employ the revolutionary
staging techniques of twentieth-century theatre.

Usually specific issues are elements of a larger intention.
Ibsen maintained that *A Doll's House* was not simply about
women's liberation, but about society's restrictions on all
people as manifested in a particular dramatic situation that
happens to focus on a woman seeking freedom from her given
role. In plays that are not intentionally and overtly didactic,

issues are usually effectively conveyed as part of the total experience the play creates, having an integral relationship with its other theatrical elements, not as isolated statements telegraphing the author's message. If you discover the only intention of a script is the airing of a specific issue, encourage the playwright either to develop a more dramatic context or to go into journalism.

Procedure

Read the script with pencil in hand. When major events or components of the story occur, tick in the margin so you can find them again. Mark character entrances, important scenes, images, *coups de theatre*, and direct statements of the play's issues.

Go back over the script, noticing your marks in the margins. Then make extensive general notes, recording your responses to the material and indicating questions you will raise with the playwright. Continue to clarify your perception of the script's intention by studying how several of its elements function.

In this reading you begin to define the world of the play in several ways. What are the given circumstances or pre-existing conditions that set up the play's events? How does the story unfold? Try to derive the internal logic in the script that governs the characters' actions and choices. Note how and where the internal logic differs from everyday reality and what rules prevail. How, for example, does time operate in the play? Are there physical disjunctions in the play's geography? If there are logical inconsistencies, do they seem to be deliberate?

Begin to identify the play's external logic by listing the major performance conventions used by the playwright. Identify any particularities of language. What style of acting is required? What is the relationship between audience and performers: Is the audience looking through a fourth wall as passive spectators? Are they being directly addressed? Are they expected to take some action during the performance? How are technical effects employed? Envision how the play will take shape on the stage and what qualities of performance it will evoke.

Write down a brief summary of the script's literal story, a step-by-step review of who does what to whom. Does the story make sense? How complete is it? How does it conform to the world of the play?

Go back over these notations and list the major events that propel the story forward. Does the story seem to flow naturally or are there gaps, redundancies, or shifts that confuse you? Pay particular attention to the places where you do not understand what is going on or lose the thread of the story. Notice which characters are central to the story and what happens to them during the play.

Determine the essential story by making a direct, succinct statement of the play's central dramatic action. What sort of story is this? Does it remind you of any generic model? Does it employ the particular conventions that usually accompany this type of narrative form? Where are the expectations established by the essential story met? Where are the deviations? What key moments are necessary for the essential story as you have defined it? What hinges the parts of the story together?

Identify issues the script raises, both as stated directly by the characters or implied by what happens in the play? List these issues and note the manner in which they are presented.

Recall what initially intrigued you about the play. Is this reinforced by a closer reading? How is your understanding of the script's intention enlarged or altered by your examination of its world, story, and issues? Note the clarifications as well as the questions raised by your analysis. Pay particular attention to discontinuities or elements of the script that do not work for you. Now it may be useful to share your discoveries with the playwright, to express how you think the script is working and, especially, to clarify whether things you do not understand are a result of your lack of perception or a result of the way the script is constructed.

Playwright/Director Meeting:
Dramaturgy, World, Story, Issues

Meeting with the playwright to discuss developmental dramaturgy gives you the opportunity to communicate what you are finding in the script and ask about areas of confusion. The playwright needs to know how the script affects you, if you understand what the play is about, and if you can help clarify and strengthen it. Probably no one but the playwright has encountered the play as minutely and as technically as you are beginning to, so he is understandably eager for response.

As you begin to work together on the script, the terms of your relationship and the nature of your collaboration on this project will evolve. You need to align your approach and your vocabulary with how the playwright works and wants to work on this particular project. Be prepared to offer a lot of response and let the playwright decide what is useful and how to apply it to his own work on the script. Again, make it clear that as a developmental director your concern is to advocate the script and work with the playwright to theatrically explore the script and bring its elements into congruence with the play's intentions.

It may be that this type of analytical discussion is not desirable or useful to the playwright. Recall Samuel Beckett's answer to director Alan Schneider's inquiries about the meanings of *Waiting for Godot*: "If I knew what it meant, I would have put it in the play." Sometimes playwrights cannot, do not, or will not talk about their plays, nor should they be required to explain what they have written according to the terms or process outlined here. However, even though you may not choose to proceed with the pencil-in-hand, sit-down dramaturgical conferences described below, you still need to find some way to ask and answer these kinds of questions. You may find that these discoveries are better made on your feet in rehearsals, or you may need to formulate these questions on your own and "discuss" them with the playwright only through the directing choices you make.

Both director and playwright approach a first dramaturgical meeting with the goal of understanding each other's responses to the script through specific discussion about the ways several of its elements operate. The following is a useful agenda:

- establish the dramaturgical vocabulary you will be using, so that you can understand each other;
- discuss the play's intention and how the intention is realized in the experience the script evokes in the theatre;
- focus on the world of the play, its story, and the issues it raises.

Remind the playwright what excites you about the script, what you perceive as its strengths, and what you like about it. Explain your sense of the play's intention and how you derived that meaning from the script. Although your mutual understanding of the intention will certainly evolve as you work together on the script, you must begin your work with a common understanding of what the playwright wants to communicate to an audience. You will present—and may argue for—your own interpretation of the play, but remember that in this kind of developmental process it is the playwright's vision that must prevail; leave it to directors of subsequent productions to invoke the "intentional fallacy" and to apply their own concepts to this material.

You and the playwright need to speak a common language about the play. Explain your methods of analysis, what terms you are using, and what they mean to you. Be prepared to adapt your vocabulary to suit the playwright's preferences.

You may call the essential story the "central dramatic action," the "spine of the play," or the "Cheez Whiz," as long as you both understand the terminology and apply it to your mutual work on the script.

Give the playwright a general response based on your reading and ask for clarification of areas that are confusing to you. The playwright may have questions for you that parallel the kinds of questions you are asking concerning the story, world of the play, issues, and what you perceive as the play's intention.

- Compare your perceptions of what the play is about with the playwright's intentions: "This is what I saw going on in the play . . . "
- Indicate major areas of obscurity, where the play does not seem to be logical, or where you just do not understand what is going on in terms of the playwright's expressed intention or the story. "I don't understand this section"; or "I was really confused when character A did such and such."
- Make note of the issues you listed in your reading and confirm them with the playwright. "At this moment in the play character C is angry because . . . " or "I thought this sequence of events expressed such and such . . . "
- Give your own impression of the world of the play by describing its internal logic—"I found a very strict hierarchy of power operating in this play," or "The environment seems like a satirical twist on the typical suburban lifestyle"—and by giving your understanding of the play's external logic: "This calls for a farcical performance style with lots of manic energy," or "The figures in black do not exist within the narrative reality, but are there to manipulate elements of the mise-en-scène."

Questions to Ask the Playwright. You might ask the playwright a series of questions with the aim of discovering what he intends the play to be and what he has done deliberately to make it that way. Again, do not argue with the playwright about what he thinks he wrote; listen and compare what he says with what you got from the script when you read it. It is useful to make notes at all meetings.

Inquire about the intention, both directly and indirectly, by asking the following kinds of questions:

- Where did you get the idea for this play?
- What is the piece about to you?
- Why did you choose this title?
- What moment, or line, or image in the play is most important?
- What do you want the audience to carry away?
- What specific issues do you address in the play?

You are not asking about the story at this point, but where the idea came from, and what the issues are to the playwright. You are trying to discover the playwright's deliberate intentions and to determine whether the play's theatrical elements manifest those intentions.

Asking about the World. Approach the world of the play by discussing the elements that define both its internal and external logics.

Internal logic:

- How would you describe the physical and social environments of the play?
- Are there rules that govern this world that I should know about?
- How is time organized in the play?
- What aspects of the play's world affect the characters' behavior?

External logic:

- How do you envision the overall performance style of the play?
- What theatrical conventions are you using?
- What is your purpose in using each one?
- What is the role of the audience for this play?

Asking about the Story. You can approach the story of the play directly, by asking the playwright what he thinks the narrative thrust is and how he has organized it:

- What is the story of the play?
- What kind of story is it?
- Where does it start and where does it end?
- What are the major things that happen in the story?
- Who is the story about?
- What happens onstage?
- What happens offstage?

These are ways of exploring the story of the piece, of determining whether it is complete, and whether there are nondeliberate gaps in the story. Sometimes, strict narrative logic simply does not apply to the larger concerns of the play. (Does it really matter whether Lady Macbeth has children? At one point in the play it is theatrically effective for her to say she has, for the rest of the play it is more important that the Macbeths are without heirs.)

Many modern scripts do not use traditionally linear stories. If this is the case, rephrase your questions to determine what the particular logic of the story is and then evaluate the other elements of the play according to that logic.

By the end of this dramaturgical session you should have a preliminary understanding of what the playwright is trying to do and how the play functions on several levels to achieve that intention. The playwright will have an initial response from you about how the play works from a director's perspective and which elements of the play you found confusing or interpreted differently than the playwright intended. Neither one of you will answer all the questions at this point. What you will do is identify areas that need further exploration.

The playwright may look at the script after this conversation with the director and consider how to proceed. Several responses are possible:

- he may feel that this director does not understand the play or communicate on a level that will stimulate fruitful collaboration;
- he may rethink how the play works, perhaps leading to new writing and new organization of the script's elements;
- he may consider how the developmental process should proceed and what resources and methods are best suited to useful work on the script.

The director should reread and rethink the play considering the playwright's stated intention. Has the script been clarified by this dramaturgical session? If your response to the play is not what the playwright intended, figure out what you missed or what made you see the play differently. Can you reconcile your perceptions with the playwright's and understand the script in his terms? If not, the playwright needs to know how you see the play and why. Let the playwright decide what kind of play it will be, and you decide whether you want to work on it.

During the dramaturgical process the playwright may come in with rewrites. If so, repeat the exploratory steps described above and convey the results of your analysis of the new material to the playwright. Consider particularly the changes and their effect on the logic, clarity, and power of the script and how the changes address the issues previously raised.

Reading for the Event Chain

> "What a strange chain of events. Why these events? Why in this order?"
>
> —Beaumarchais, *The Marriage of Figaro*

An *event* in a script is a related sequence of stage activity that forms an identifiable unit of action. Events are distinguished by transitions, which occur when there is a change of direction in a scene, usually brought about by the entrance of a new character or the introduction of a new piece of information. These transitions create links between one event and the next. The linked series of theatrical moments—the event chain—creates the dynamic shape of the play: how the playwright has ordered the material.

A script's events move the other theatrical elements forward through time and space, leading to what J. L. Styan calls the "plotted sequence of impressions" upon an audience. Identifying and understanding a script's events and their particular order reveals not only the shape of the play but often the shape of your work on the play as well. Event analysis looks at a script to see what happens, in what sequence it happens, and what the relationship is between happenings.

Director Alan Schneider talks about event analysis in these terms: "I'm looking for changes of relationship between the characters, between a character and his environment, between one element and another. I break up the script into something happening, and then something else happening, and then something else happening. . . . Anything to give the performer some sense of structure or form or sequence, that's what you want."[2]

Event analysis is always interpretational: when you analyze the event structure of a script you are stating how you see the play unfolding in performance. You are not identifying what is inherently there but rather *what you perceive to be there.* When you convey your event analysis to the playwright you are describing how you envision the moment-to-moment progression of the play. How closely your interpretation coincides with his intention reveals either how well he has accomplished what he undertook or how much you missed in your analysis.

As the director you must figure out how the event structure

---

2. R. H. O'Neill, *The Director as Artist* (New York: Holt, Rinehart & Winston, 1987), 118.

of the script operates, because the events form the units of work accomplished in staging the script. At some point in the rehearsal process, even in the most seemingly disjointed or collage-structured play, the events must be put in a sequence that best serves the script's intention. Usually the playwright arrives with a script in which the nature and sequence of the events are fairly set, although some writers create fragments and look to the developmental process as an opportunity to put pieces of the script together and experiment with different combinations to see what happens.

There is an important distinction between theatrical events (the linked chain of one-after-the-other happenings described above) and narrative events. Narrative events are episodes of the story that can include offstage action, such as the auction of the estate in *The Cherry Orchard*, or events that take place before the beginning of the play, such as the sacrifice of Iphigeneia and history of the Trojan war before Agamemnon's return in *The Oresteia*.

Your analysis of story and world of the play (see above) examines the narrative events and looks for discontinuities to see whether they are intentional or not. Examining the logic of the story often raises questions about the sequence of the event chain. For example, does it make sense for Yolanda to confront Fred about his infidelity if the story has not previously set up the opportunity for her to make this discovery? Possibly not, although some plays, like Pinter's *Betrayal* or Churchill's *Top Girls*, alter the chronology of the story so the chain of events proceeds in a different sequence from the narrative. Such apparent discontinuities are, in fact, intentional in these scripts.

With an understanding of the distinction between the story and the chain of events as the play unfolds moment-to-moment in the theatre, examine the relationship between the two. Most plays are linear and causal in their event structure, so that the progression of stage action also unfolds the narrative or tells the story, mirroring our perception (or perhaps our hope) that life proceeds in a similarly logical manner.[3]

When the narrative progression is altered or subsumed by an event chain that proceeds according to something other than the sequential episodes of the story, plays can create nonlinear patterns, linking events according to their own systems of organization: the dialectical argument in Brecht's *The Measures Taken*; the mental triggering of one image by another in the works of Robert Wilson; the circular repetitions of anticipation and despair in *Waiting for Godot*; the warps of time, culture, character identity, and gender in Churchill's *Cloud Nine*; the collage of evidence in Weiss's *The Investigation*; or the flow of character revelations in Shange's *For Colored Girls Who Have Considered Suicide When the Rainbow Is Enuf*.

Whether or not the onstage events are chronological episodes of the story, they are causal from the audience point of view. That is, the audience first sees one thing happen, then a second, then a third, and so on. No matter what the sequence, audiences look for a specific, though not always realistic, logic ordering the events and determining the shape of the play. Each event must move the play forward, with the

---

3. David Ball's *Backwards and Forwards: A Technical Manual for Reading Plays* (Carbondale: Southern Illinois University Press, 1983) is an excellent guide to linear event analysis. It explains his useful idea of the twofold nature of an action and of the causal connections between successive domino-like progressions of events through a script, which he calls "triggers and heaps." Everything that happens in a script is the result of a previous event and the cause of the next. According to Ball, the clearest way to identify the causal connections in a script is to begin with the final event and to trace the causes backwards to the beginning of the play. As a result, each event is analyzed with the knowledge of where it is leading. For example, in *Hamlet* the soldiers bear the body of Hamlet away because Fortinbras has so ordered; Fortinbras gives the order because Horatio has suggested performing the appropriate rites before he tells the story of what has taken place; Horatio makes the suggestion because Hamlet's dying request was for him to pass on the story; and so on, backwards through the script to the first trigger: Bernardo's fearful "Who's there?" spoken because of the pre-play given circumstances of a dark night on a lonely battlement in a politically and supernaturally troubled kingdom.

specific sequence and sum of events creating an affective experience for the audience. The director's job is to understand how the progression of the script operates and how the chain of events will be orchestrated in the theatre, asking Figaro's questions: "Why these events? Why in this order?"

Procedure

Derive the event chain of the play by performing an event analysis.

The first step in identifying the event structure of a script is to get a general sense of the movement of the whole play. What is the essential story that the play presents? (Oedipus discovers the truth about who he is, or Mother Courage loses her children, Prince Hal wins his place as England's glorious king.) Next, focus on how the play unfolds moment to moment.

Identify the major events. The easiest way to isolate events is to mark the script where you perceive a major shift during the scene. By doing this you locate the links or transitions between the events of the chain; the events themselves fall between the transitions. Some transitions are easy to identify. There is always a transition at a scene break. Generally, character entrances and exits mark transitions and the French scenes[4] between these transitions are events.

Go back over the script and look closely at what happens within each event. Write down a one-sentence description of each event. You will derive a list of the main things that happen in the play thus: *David enters; he accuses Sarah of infidelity; she takes out a gun; he tries to placate her; she shoots him.* Be careful that you write down only the main events; you will have a tendency to write down everything: *David enters; he mentions the weather; Sarah asks him if he is thirsty; he requests a cup of*

---

4. So-called because in the French Neoclassical tradition scene breaks are indicated with every entrance or exit of a character.

tea; she asks him if he had a good time last night; he explains his family's reaction to fog. In this example nothing after *David enters* is an event because the stages of the conversation do not really contribute anything to the forward motion of the scene, as revealing as they might be of character or world of the play or previous circumstances.

It is also possible to isolate too few events. *The men gather on the battlement* and *The Ghost silently appears* are certainly two of the major events in the first scene of *Hamlet,* but important events occur between the two that need to be identified to distinguish a complete event chain. If you overlook Horatio's expressed doubts about the veracity of the Ghost you miss the establishment of Horatio's function as a truth teller (he is left at the end of the play to tell Hamlet's story to Fortinbras and the world) and you miss the script's logical reason for the Ghost's first appearance: to convince Horatio—and the audience—that he exists. This produces Horatio's questioning of the Ghost; the Ghost's subsequent silence provokes Horatio to inform Hamlet of the mysterious event, and the play's events are off and running.

After identifying the events, reexamine the transitions between them. Figure out what causes each transition and what happens as a result of it. This step forces you to reexamine the event chain and helps ensure that the units you isolated as events are actually events.

At this stage of your analysis you may have one of several situations. You may derive a more-or-less complete causal sequence, in which you recognize the events as a domino-like progression of action with each event logically produced by the last and leading to the next. You may find that the events are nontraditional: they may be images, or a series of apparently unlinked monologues as in *Kennedy's Children,* or a repeating cycle of actions told each time from a new perspective as in *Rashomon.* The event chain is what it is, and you must not try to force it into a predetermined model.

To test whether the event chain is effective, examine it in terms of the world of the play and its story. The event analysis may reveal discontinuities and lack of connections that are entirely appropriate to the world that the playwright is creating: in such scripts discontinuities and lack of causality are entirely deliberate and must be respected. In most linear scripts, however, they are not intentional; the playwright thinks he has written a causal event chain.

If this is the case, look for discontinuities and jumps, missing causes or effects, off-the-wall events, and deus ex machinae. Your analysis may also reveal nondeliberate redundancies in the event chain. You may discover that Susan spurns William three times, when once would be plenty. (Alternately, the three repetitions of this single event may be deliberate, with the intention of invoking St. Peter's three denials of Christ.) Ideally, each event, even a repetitive event, will be different enough from the others to add a layer of complexity to the script and to keep it moving forward.

Alternately, if event-chain analysis reveals deliberate non-causality, the playwright is working in a nonlinear mode. In this case, investigate the function of each segment in relation to the larger whole without getting too caught up in linear causality. Each segment should do something different and progressive in terms of the cumulative impact of the play. If causality is not moving the play forward, what is? For example, in Christofer's *The Shadow Box*, the events are linked in a thematic procession; Strindberg's *Ghost Sonata* moves according to the free associations of the dreamer; *Death of a Salesman* unfolds both narratively and expressionistically, revealing through stage action the progressive unraveling of a character's mind.

Create a list of the play's events, or make an event-chain chart, so you can show the playwright your interpretation. (Figure 3.1 presents a simplified event-chain chart for Synge's *Riders to the Sea*.)

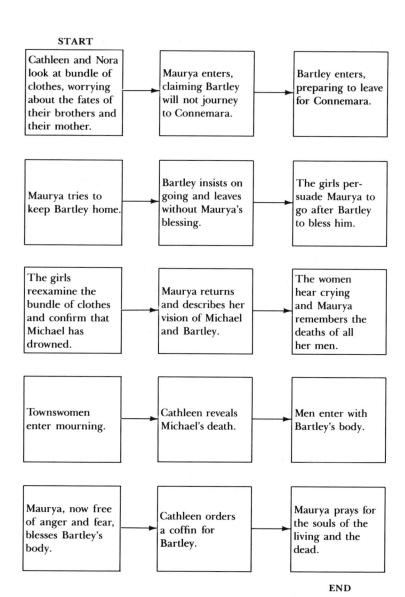

START

Cathleen and Nora look at bundle of clothes, worrying about the fates of their brothers and their mother. → Maurya enters, claiming Bartley will not journey to Connemara. → Bartley enters, preparing to leave for Connemara.

Maurya tries to keep Bartley home. → Bartley insists on going and leaves without Maurya's blessing. → The girls persuade Maurya to go after Bartley to bless him.

The girls reexamine the bundle of clothes and confirm that Michael has drowned. → Maurya returns and describes her vision of Michael and Bartley. → The women hear crying and Maurya remembers the deaths of all her men.

Townswomen enter mourning. → Cathleen reveals Michael's death. → Men enter with Bartley's body.

Maurya, now free of anger and fear, blesses Bartley's body. → Cathleen orders a coffin for Bartley. → Maurya prays for the souls of the living and the dead.

END

Figure 3.1. Event analysis of *Riders to the Sea*, by John Millington Synge, 1904

This chart gives you something concrete to discuss with the playwright. You may discover in your conversation with the playwright that you have missed or overlooked important events or that you have isolated things that he did not intend to function as events. Your event analysis should also reveal the overall dynamic shape of the play (discussed in more detail under "Reading for Patterns," below).

Playwright/Director Meeting: Events

For the Director. Go over the event analysis with the playwright. By now you have a detailed understanding of how the events of the script conjoin. Because you are looking at it with a director's eye and not from inside the playwright's head, you may be able to tell the playwright things about the script he did not realize or did not intend.

Refrain from offering corrective criticism. Again, report to the playwright what your analysis revealed and check to see that your analysis confirms his intentions. If it does not, you must reexamine your analysis, just as the playwright must reexamine his execution of the expressed intention. In these instances, simply asking about the jumps in causality or redundancies may be all the comment a playwright needs to rethink the material. Remember, it is important to keep from offering specific fixes, especially in the early days.

After you go over the event chain with the playwright, indicate where there are knots in your perception, or fuzziness, where you do not understand why a particular event is in the script, or what makes events change, or whether the omission of causality is deliberate, or how we get from A to J.

For the Playwright. This is an opportunity for the writer to have a more specific response on how the play works moment-to-moment, as it does in the theatre. Event analysis is not a science but a matter of perception. If the director overlooked a major development or obsesses on inconsequential activities, this is the time to examine the basis of those perceptions. Writers may inform the director of these missed moments and discuss how they work. The director may then say, "Of course, I see now, that's obvious: the turning point in the scene is where Rochelle picks up the letter."

If the director remains confused about the progression of events, then the writer may examine the script to see if the necessary indicators are present or if the event is genuinely missing or misplaced. The priority is to make sure that there is a clear record in the script of the writer's intentions, so that subsequent directors can work without the playwright's personal explanations.

Generally, these are the kinds of things to check:

- Examine the event chain to make sure the key events are present to articulate the story or express a dramatic action;
- See that necessary causes and effects are clear, yet compelling;
- Question whether the events are consistent with the world of the play;
- Examine how the events express the issues of the piece;
- Look at how much of the action takes place onstage and how much offstage;
- Look at how much is said and not done. Onstage action is generally more interesting than description of offstage events.

Often a major rewrite occurs after close analysis of the events. When you get the new material, repeat what you did in the previous reading: analyze the event chain and look for clarity in the execution of the script's intention. Remember that as you cut through layers of obscurity in the script increasingly subtle things will reveal themselves. Allow your understanding of the script to change as the script changes; do not cling to an earlier form if that is no longer appropriate.

As you work on event analysis, keep in mind Linda Lavin's description of a good director, spoken during the 1988 Tony awards presentation: "A good director maps out the route and goes the journey with you."

Reading for Characters

Characters are the agents of the play's events and the use of characters in action is the playwright's essential theatrical element. Character analysis examines why and how these particular characters are in this play, looking at character function, the relationship web, each character's event chain, and their individual characteristics.

Character Function. Each character has a place in the overall event chain and, through various means, contributes to the play's intention. Character function is the theatrical need that compels the playwright's creation of the character—the structural reason for the character's presence in the script. A character may function as a provider of exposition like Petterson in Ibsen's *The Wild Duck*, a personification of a moral force like Aphrodite in Euripides' *Hippolytus*, an antagonist like the Cardinal in Webster's *The Duchess of Malfi*, a scapegoat like Karl Hudlocke in Durang's *The Marriage of Bette and Boo*, an everyman like Emily in Wilder's *Our Town*, a piece of scenery like the bohemian peasants in *The Winter's Tale*, or a fragmented aspect of another character like Jim or Nell in Nichols's *Passion*. Characters should serve at least one function; they may have several.

Relationship Web. In most plays, characters are connected and their behavior toward each other is determined by the terms of their relationships. This principle of the relationship web in human interaction is aptly described by anthropologist Victor Turner: "If we are, visibly, islands, we are genetically and culturally linked by ties of love and hate, by the pleasure bond, the pain bond, by the duty chain, by *noblesse oblige*, or by the innate or induced needs for dominance or submission.

We are for, against, with, toward, above, below, within, outside, or without one another."[5]

While the audience encounters the characters only from curtain to curtain, within the narrative world of the play the characters are usually joined before the action begins by the given circumstances, including preexisting relationships involving family, social, political, emotional or situational ties. When the play begins there are already tensions within the web that are revealed through the exposition, the ways characters respond to one another, and what they say about each other. Hamlet's "a little more than kin, and less than kind" reveals, in his first utterance, a powerful preexisting tension in the relationship web linking him to Claudius, Gertrude, and his dead father.

The progress of the play's events generates an evolving tension within the web, creating dynamic interactions whereby the movement of any character has an impact on others in the web—this is often the source of the dramatic conflict. In Sartre's *No Exit*, Garcin refers to this tension when he says, "They have laid their snare damned cunningly—like a cobweb. If you make any movement, if you raise your hand to fan yourself, Estelle and I feel a little tug ... we're linked together inextricably."[6] In the course of the play, characters form and dissolve alliances and undergo internal and external transformations that change their relationships to those around them; new characters are introduced who affect the dynamic of the web, and usually the external forces of fate or history or the local gods exert their influence on the network of relationships.

---

5. Victor Turner, "Liminality and the Performative Genres," in *Rite, Drama, Festival, Spectacle: Rehearsals Toward a Theory of Cultural Performance*, ed. John J. MacAloon (Philadelphia: Institute for the Study of Human Issues, 1984), 19.

6. Jean-Paul Sartre, *No Exit and Three Other Plays* (New York: Vintage Books, 1955), 29.

Character Event Chains. A character's event chain maps his or her progress through the play. An analysis of what happens to a character from moment to moment reveals that character's function, decisions, obstacles, adjustments, and the impact of changing circumstances. Most plays depict a character's journey from one condition to another, impelled by the events of the play.

As with the event chain of the entire play, there should be an internal logic controlling the character's movement from one event link to the next. This logic should be consistent with the overall world of the play. Another way to think of the character event chain is as an individual instrumental part of an orchestral score; the actors must be able to play their roles both for themselves and in concert with the other performers.

Individual Characteristics. These are the self-contained elements of personality and appearance specific to each character. Distinctive qualities of speech, physicality, and emotional and intellectual responses describe individual characters and affect audience perceptions about who these people are and what they are doing. These internal and external characteristics serve as the bases for an actor's exploration of the psychology and physicality of the role.

Procedure

Complete a detailed character analysis, examining functions, relationship web, individual event chains, and individual characteristics.

Determine the function or functions of each character by asking how and why the characters contribute to the overall intention of the play. Look for characters who have no function, repetitive characters, missing characters, and characters who disappear part way through. You may find extra characters or not enough characters. Ask the following questions:

- How does each character's actions help shape the overall event chain?
- How does the script induce your responses to each character, and are those responses consistent?
- If there are several characters serving one function, is it that way for a reason?

Make sure you understand the relationship web, concentrating on the characters' relationships to the other characters and how the relationships change throughout the play. Here are two simple but useful techniques for approaching the relationship web: first, create a character chart, listing characters across the top and down the side of a page and specifying each character's relationships to all the others: define the relationship between Character A and Character B, between Character A and Character C, and so on. Then draw out a relationship web or series of webs using and labeling lines showing the proximities, ties, and tensions between individual characters and/or groups of characters and illustrating how they change as the play progresses. Look for the causes of change and the results of it. A play may begin with one character in the center of the web and end with another in that position. This reordering of the play's relationships may or may not be in accord with the playwright's intention. You may discover discontinuities, gaps, or snarls in the web, which either you or the writer need to address.

As you did for the whole script, derive the event chain for each character. Look for the relationship between the individual and the overall event chains. Check each event chain to learn if and how the characters change throughout the play. Notice the connection between the individual event chains and the relationship web.

Examine the individual characteristics of each character, looking for signs—Richard's hump, Blanche's self-deception,

Eliott's quick wit, Pale's manic speech patterns, Stanley's glasses, Hermione's generosity of spirit—of who these people are and how their characteristics connect with what they do and what the play is about:

- Has the playwright indicated particular physicalities for any of the characters? Are these integral to the intention and the events of the script?
- Do the characters possess individuality of thought process, reaction, and behavior?
- Are the characters' psychologies, motivational structures, and responses to events as complex as is appropriate for the particular play?
- Are character responses consistent within the character's psychology or function?
- Are the characters plausible in terms of the world of the play?
- Are they predictable?
- Does each character speak with an individual voice? Is that individual voice consistent with the voice of the larger play?
- Are the characters actable, that is, has the playwright provided a foundation for the actors' work that does not restrict their contribution in creating the character?
- Why do we care or not care about the characters?

The precise nature of the characters depends upon the world of the play, which may dictate whether the characters are cartoon cutouts, psychologically complex personalities, or abstract representations. Once you have determined the kind of beings likely to inhabit the world of this play you can begin to focus on whether the characters are consistent with that environment, true to their own characteristics, and supportive of the script's intentions.

Playwright/Director Meeting: Characters

Discuss your character analysis in terms of function, relationship web, individual characteristics, and each character's progression through the play. Indicate how you think each character functions in the script and the connections of those functions to the overall event chain and the play's intention. Explore how each character is defined in terms of physicality, diction, responses, and motivation. Examine the bonds between characters, how they are established and how they change over the course of the play. If you perceive troublesome acting problems in any of the characters (for example, unmotivated behavior, inconsistent individual characteristics, awkward speech patterns), mention them, but be sure to note that actors should speak to these issues.

This may be a good time to have a preliminary discussion about casting. Ask the playwright whether there are specific actors or types of actors who possess the qualities, energies, and technical abilities suited to his vision of the characters and the world they inhabit. Share your own thoughts about casting and use this discussion to further explore the requirements of each role and whether the characters derived from the text conform with what the playwright says he wants.

Often your responses will enlarge or even change the playwright's ideas about who these characters are. If you cannot find evidence to support the playwright's conception of each role, you should point that out and look again for signs you may have missed. The playwright may also consider your difficulty and look at the way the characters are drawn and how a clearer record of his intentions might be inscribed, particularly for later productions that will cast the roles without the benefit of his participation.

Your analysis and this discussion of the characters should help you understand how the playwright wants the characters to operate in the script. As with your earlier dramaturgical session, exploring these issues may lead the playwright to make revisions in the script or at least identify areas that require further attention as the developmental work continues. Remember that character, like all categories of dramaturgical analysis, cannot be separated from the other elements in a script; as you focus on understanding how the characters work, you continue to examine the world of the play, its story and issues, always guided by the play's intentions.

Reading for Patterns

There is something about human perception that causes us to look for patterns and derive meaning from the models of reality they suggest. The playwright often, perhaps inevitably, organizes theatrical elements in patterns, creating points of reference, repetition, contrast, and comparison. Patterns expressed in the theatrical event are inherently powerful and must be understood and tested against the intention of the play.

Sometimes the patterns of a play are linked to larger cultural or universal patterns. There may be physical, visual, or verbal allusions to the cycle of seasons, the ages of man, death and renewal, darkness and light, male and female, young and old, passion and restraint. Patterns of social behavior, political processes, music, or natural phenomena may underlie a play's events, ideas, character web, imagery, rhythms, and language. Assumptions about the progress of history, the evolution of species, or the formless absurdity of it all may be reflected in the play's organization of its elements.

Patterns of Events. Within the script, the patterns of events can be seen as the general dynamic shape of the event chain, which may be arranged in any way: as a domino-like sequence of physical actions building to a climax and ending with a resolution and denouement; as a circular pattern of repetition; as variations on a theme; as a series of tangential explorations; or any other method or methods of event organization that serve the play's intention and provoke audience interest.

A pattern frequently found in Shakespeare's history plays, for example, is the pattern of the wheel of fortune— elevating one king, only to bring him around to disaster as another rises to take his place. Similarly, the Greek tragic dramatists sometimes used the pattern of the great person brought down, gaining self-knowledge in the process. Structural anthropologists such as Gilbert Murray, Victor Turner, and others have theorized universal ritual patterns found in diverse societies and reflected in the structures of dramatic performance.

Not all patterns are linear and causal. In Robert Wilson's *Einstein on the Beach*, for example, the pattern of events mirrors the series of synapse-like images that flashed into Wilson's head inspired by the concepts of time, space, and Einstein's biography. Given the quantum-mechanical nature of Wilson's subject, something other than linearity in the pattern of events was appropriate. In *Blue Window*, by Craig Lucas, the patterns are in the form of a mosaic of an event—the party—and the revelations of the characters' personal histories and relationships. As the party proceeds, each of the characters' identities is pointillistically revealed by scenes and monologues that exist outside the event structure of what happens at the party itself.

In Albee's *Who's Afraid of Virginia Woolf?* there are several patterns in the structure of the event chain. There is a journey into—and through—the night, marked by a series of party games ("Get the Guests," "Humiliate the Host," "Hump the Hostess," and "Bringing up Baby"). A further pattern in the event chain is the series of boxing-match-like "rounds" between George and Martha, some of them even punctuated by the ringing of a bell. Here is a pattern of events interwoven with a pattern of physical action and a pattern of sounds.

Patterns are also evident in the shape of individual character event chains. The pattern of Macbeth's actions charts his descent into dehumanization. Ibsen's *Ghosts* manifests the pattern of Mrs. Alving's tortured progress toward the freedom and terror of personal responsibility. Brecht's *Good Person of Setzuan* shows Shin Te's vicious cycle of generosity and greed.

Patterns of Time. The way time works in the play often determines the shape and patterns of events. A script may adhere to a rational time frame in which the events and chronology are equivalent with the stage time in the theatre. A script may represent a reverse or altered chronology as in Pinter's *Betrayal*, in which the scenes are presented not in the order in which they chronologically occurred but rather in the order 8, 9, 7, 6, 3, 4, 5, 2, 1, creating a pattern that critic Martin Esslin says "represents changes in our minds as we look back on what happened."[7] In Churchill's *Top Girls*, the first scene exists out of the narrative time frame entirely, bringing diverse characters together for a fantasy dinner party, and the final scene of the play is actually the first scene in terms of its chronological order. (Churchill has said that this ability to play with time is one of the things she loves about the theatre.) A play may proceed through the same time frame from different perspectives as in Brecht's *Caucasian Chalk Circle*. It may follow an epic time frame covering many centuries, or have no basis in rational time, creating an absurd world in which time itself takes on relative, if any, meaning.

Character Patterns. A play's patterns may be detected in the juxtaposition of characters, such as the three vengeful sons Hamlet, Laertes, and Fortinbras, or the repetition of character actions like Oswald's echo of his father's "joy of life" in *Ghosts*. In *The Shadow Box*, three sets of otherwise unrelated characters face terminal illness. The patterned juxtapositions between these characters provide a way to make intellectual and emotional comparisons.

Image Patterns. Many scripts contain patterns of images that reinforce the intention and help articulate the elements. Image patterns are often essential to understanding the logic of the play, the individual characteristics of its people, and even the organization of the event chain.

---

7. Martin Esslin, *Pinter the Playwright* (London: Metheun and Co., 1984), 206.

In *Macbeth*, for example, the image of blood is a crucial element in the world of the play. The first human figure seen by the audience is the "Bloody Sergeant," who arrives to tell the bloody deeds of Macbeth's heroism; the physical presence of blood runs through the play from Macbeth's dagger to Banquo's ghost to Lady Macbeth's stained hands to the final bloodletting of Macbeth's defeat. This image pattern is also a guide to that play's pattern of events; "blood will have blood," Macbeth says, and the acceleration of violence happens because of the uncontrollable consequences of assassination. Macbeth's personal journey through the play can also be charted in terms of the image pattern. He wades into blood until it cuts him off from any vestiges of his civilized humanity and finally drowns him.

The use of image patterns allows the introduction of large ideas and referents that can help make the play work on multiple levels: consider the nets in *Agamemnon*, the glass menagerie, or the cherry orchard as images that expand the audience's experience of the play.

Patterns of Language. Language, of course, is a principal source for pattern analysis, particularly as it expresses a character's spoken actions. Individuals speak in different ways and for different reasons, depending on what they are trying to do, what they are reacting to, their world, and their individual characteristics. The distinctive patterns of each character's language are important ways the characters reveal themselves to the audience.

Like each character, a play as a whole has its own distinctive voice, its language, which is a major contributor to the creation of the world of the play. Sometimes playwrights deliberately use language that would not ordinarily be used by characters in such a situation: Caryl Churchill's use of rhyming couplets in *Serious Money* distances us from the world of high finance and allows us to view it objectively; Alan Bowne creates what is essentially a new language in *Beirut*, as do Jim Cartwright in *Road* and Steven Berkoff in *East*. In these cases the idiosyncratic language patterns reveal exceptional worlds and they literally speak to audiences in distinctive ways.

Whether it is in the regularity and rhymes of the French alexandrine in Racine's *Phaedre*, the brittle word games of *Private Lives*, the refrain of "Let's go" in *Waiting for Godot*, or the gloomy repetition of Macbeth's "If it were done when 'tis done, then 'twere well / It were done quickly," the patterns of language enunciate the world of the play and, along with the patterns of sight, sound, and movement, create the musical qualities of rhythm and tempo that audiences respond to and directors must grasp.

Procedure

With pattern analysis you are beginning to step away from the individual elements and starting to look at how they function together. As you reread the play, look specifically for its patterns and how they support the play's intention. Your earlier analyses will contain much of this information.

Charting the shape of the event chain is a helpful way to discover patterns of action. A traditional method of arranging the event chain is to construct a fever chart reflecting the rising and falling action of the play, as shown in figure 3.2. Remember that an event chain chart may assume any shape; there is no correct or proper shape. You are looking for deliberate or nondeliberate patterns or repetitions in the events or in their dynamics.

The event chain analysis will also help you understand the script's temporal organization. A useful technique is to isolate the play's events and arrange or rearrange them in real-time or causal chronological order. Then compare that order to the theatrical order of events that the playwright is using. If you discover that the pattern of events depicts a nonlinear time structure, then you must explore how that structure supports the play's intention. For example, Churchill's *Top Girls*,

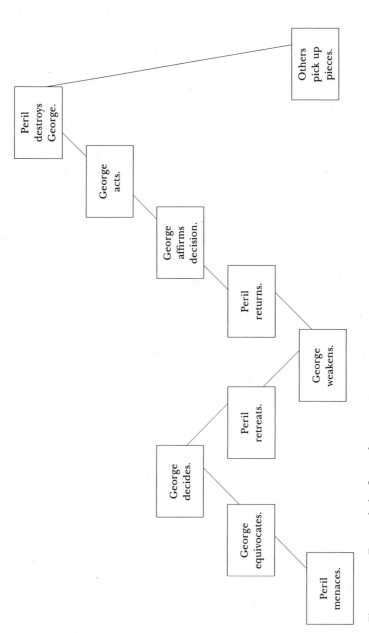

Figure 3.2. Event chain fever chart

where the final scene of the play is in fact the first chronological scene in the story, has the effect of causing the audience to reevaluate the characters' actions in the earlier scenes in light of the later revelations. The time structure of the play is archaeological or psychoanalytic: the playwright presents behavior and then examines its roots. The main body of *The Caucasian Chalk Circle* employs another kind of temporal organization: the same sequence of events is presented twice, from two different points of view; this supports Brecht's intention that there is no objective truth, but rather differing character reactions to circumstances.

Charting the individual character event chains will reveal character behavior patterns. Comparing all the character event chains will show where characters follow similar courses and where different characters vary the pattern.

Examine the relationship web for patterns. Look for repeating sets of characters like fathers and sons, persecutors and victims, or lovers. Then notice how the sets of relationship patterns in the web interact. For example, once you notice the three sets of fathers and sons in *Hamlet*, you pay attention to how they compare and contrast.

After identifying the patterns in the overall and individual event chains and in the relationship web, step back and see whether these patterns conform to larger archetypal or other familiar patterns. Understanding the play's use of prototypical patterns can be helpful in predicting how the audience is likely to react to the material. Also, consider how the distinctive patterns of this individual play will affect an audience.

As you read, make a list of recurring images and their variations:

- Are certain images associated with particular characters?
- Are certain images associated with particular events?
- Does the use of images expand your understanding of the play's intention?
- Do the images change as the play progresses?

- Are the images integral to the action of the play or do they seem to be gratuitous?

Look for the ways in which language patterns are expressed, both in the overall play and in the individual character diction. It is sometimes useful to cover up the character names and see whether you can tell who is speaking without identification.

- Is the language of each character consistent with his or her individual characteristics?
- Does character language reflect emotional state and changes?
- Is the language speakable?
- Does the language of the overall play support the world of the play and emanate from it?

Playwright/Director Meeting: Patterns

Discuss with the playwright your perceptions of the play's patterns and how they work. Three things can happen: (1) you will identify patterns that the playwright deliberately used; (2) you will have missed existing patterns; or (3) you will have picked up patterns the playwright did not know were there. The issue is again one of intentionality: Are the patterns there for a reason? What effects are they likely to have? Are these the desired effects?

Thinking about patterns is often when your own creative impulses as a director begin to flow. You may begin to specifically envision the play in terms of staging, ground plan, builds, juxtapositions, colors, and tempos. This may be a good time to share these specific impulses with the playwright and discuss the ways you are seeing the play live theatrically.

By now your dramaturgical analyses and discussions with the writer will make issues, story, events, characters, patterns, and an initial sense of the play's world apparent to you. You are getting to know the play and the playwright is getting to know your responses to it. The playwright may come in with rewrites during this process. At this point you both should review all your earlier work to see what has changed and to see whether you are moving in a direction acceptable to the playwright and appropriate for what he is trying to do with the script.

Reading for Experience

Once the playwright believes he has a satisfactory draft, you must approach the script afresh and try to encounter the *experience* of the play. Put aside your close-reading techniques, allow your eyes to shift slightly out of focus, and read the play as though you were seeing it in performance. Make few, if any, notes as you read. Allow the play to act on your perceptive and experiential mind, leaving your analytical mind out of the process as much as possible. You are looking for the fullness of the play's impressions this time, not specifics. By now you should be familiar enough with the script to begin to understand how the play will communicate as a theatrical experience. And you and the playwright should now agree on the basics: you should have a mutual understanding of the playwright's intentions in writing the play and of how the play uses the various theatrical elements to achieve the intentions.

When you finish reading, have a cup of tea and muse. Reground yourself in the play's strengths and in what attracted you to it initially. How does the play now compare to what it was when you first encountered it? Has your dramaturgical work on the play strengthened and clarified it?

Now is the time to consider what to do next:

- Your work on the script may not have been helpful to the playwright, in which case you should apologize and retire.
- The play may be stronger than it was initially but still needs further clarification and refinement; in this case you may wish to go back and repeat the appropriate analyses and discussions, work on it in different ways, or bring in someone else to look at the material.
- You and the playwright may agree that the dramaturgical

process has been fruitful and that you want to take further developmental steps. If so, it is time to bring actors into the process.

If you achieve these mutual understandings, you are ready at this stage to cast actors, add their collaborative efforts to the developmental process, and undertake whatever developmental steps you agree are next. At the very least, arrange an unrehearsed reading with competent actors so the playwright and you can hear what you have. It would not be a good idea to continue further without hearing the material.

4 · THE UNREHEARSED

READING

No MATTER how much dramaturgical analysis you apply to a script, your best information about how the play works as performance comes from hearing it read aloud. The simplest way to hear a script aloud is to have actors read it in an *unrehearsed reading*. In an unrehearsed reading you begin to understand how the script functions as a point of departure for actors and as a potential experience for an audience, even if that audience is only the playwright and director. The unrehearsed reading may be your first encounter with the play or it may be a step to which you return one or more times throughout the developmental process. Because it serves as a field test, it is a useful step after preliminary dramaturgical work.

Be aware of the limitations inherent in an unrehearsed reading. Playwrights often find them discouraging because they offer such an unrefined presentation of the script. Directors should be cognizant of this and help frame appropriate expectations from, and responses to, the reading accounting for the fact that it is only a preliminary exploration of the script as performance. Many of a script's most potent elements will not be exposed in a reading of any kind, and everyone involved must understand that a reading explores some aspects of a script and not others. It is best to approach the reading with specific and limited questions in mind, rather than as a make-or-break debut of the play. How do actors work with the material? Does the play consistently create its world? How does the script work dynamically? How does its logic operate? Does the story make sense? Were your initial responses to the script valid in this new context of even limited performance?

The unrehearsed reading requires a minimum of one session. During the reading the actors sit in chairs and hold scripts. If actors have the script a day or two in advance they can begin to formulate the broad outlines of character and relationships; they will also bring to the reading a sense of what they have already found in the script. If the actors read the script cold, they generally go with their instincts and their moment-to-moment discoveries.

WHAT THE DIRECTOR DOES

Before the reading, decide which stage directions are needed to understand the action; appoint someone, perhaps the stage manager or the script assistant, but not the director or the playwright, to read them. Only read descriptions of major stage actions, technical effects, and anything else that is absolutely necessary (*a shooting star blazes across the sky*). Leave out specific acting directions (*sadly, pointedly, with clenched teeth*). If the actors can "act" the directions (*raising a hand threateningly*), you may wish to have them do so: underline those actions that you want actors to perform. You can handle entrances and exits in a number of ways: by having them read as stage directions; by having the actor actually enter or exit the reading space as the character; or by having the actor sit forward in her chair and engage her attention in the scene for an entrance, or sit back and drop her eyes for an exit.

Try to give the actors your sense of the world of the play. Tell them that you are interested in what they discover about the characters and the script so you will let them find their own way, without much help. Ask them to keep mental notes throughout the reading of their questions and reactions.

Try to arrange the actors at the reading in a way that serves the character patterns of the script, generally in an arc so that you can see them all and so that characters who interact can see each other. Place major characters in the center, and minor characters toward the sides. If the character structure is large and relationships are complex, arrange family or relationship units together: Montagues on the left, Capulets on the right. Place the person reading stage directions slightly off to one side away from the actors. If the play requires it, change the physical placement of the actors to reflect changes in the script—perhaps during act or scene breaks, where such changes will not interfere with the reading.

The unrehearsed reading can be extremely useful with or without an audience. Often the playwright prefers to have no audience present, because just hearing actors read the text can provide all the information he needs about what to work on next. If there is an audience, introduce the reading by announcing the play's title and author; identify the characters, their relationships, and the actors playing the roles; give the time and place settings of the action; explain that the script assistant will read the stage directions.

You may wish to take notes during the reading, or tick your script to remind yourself where things occurred to you, or just sit back and experience the play as an audience member would. In any of these cases, it is a good idea to record your reactions while they are still fresh in your mind. Time the reading.

Your main job at the unrehearsed reading is to listen carefully and with great concentration. Remain neutral so that you can hear what is there and gauge the responses to the script.

Instructions to give the actors:

• Do not add any movement to the script, unless the director has asked for entrances and exits.

- Perform only those actions that are underlined in the stage directions.
- When stage directions are read, acknowledge them in your acting, so that the next thing you say is infused with the action of the stage direction and with the character's awareness of what has happened.
- Do not add voices or ornamentations unless the script specifically calls for them.
- Interact with and respond to the other actors as much as possible.[1]
- Play what is in the script and play it strongly. Let the words guide you. If the text does not tell you what to do, then remain neutral.
- Speak the words as written by the playwright (recall Hamlet's advice).

WHAT YOU LEARN FROM THE UNREHEARSED READING

The most important things you learn from the unrehearsed reading are how the script begins to create a theatrical experience and how actors respond to the material.

You will also begin to understand:

---

1. A good technique for this, time permitting, is to take the actors through a preliminary read-through using the following exercise:

Look at your script and "grab" as many words as you can comfortably hold in your memory; look into your scene partner's eyes and say your words (if you can only remember three or four words, that is fine); look back down at your script, grab a few more words, look up, and proceed through the scene in this way. Do not say anything unless you are looking at your scene partner and she is looking at you. The partner's responsibility in this exercise is always to look at the actor who is speaking while she is speaking. Grab your own words only between lines or speeches.

Because this exercise distorts the length of the script and its rhythmical structure, it seems cumbersome to the actors until they get used to it. It works best as a rehearsal technique. Actors who are skilled at unrehearsed readings do this as a matter of course.

- a general idea of the dynamic shape of the whole script;
- how the actors work with the character's events, relationships, and individual characteristics;
- whether the play's logic is consistent and convincing;
- what the action/speech balance is;
- how the patterns operate and whether or not they reinforce the intention;
- where your attention flags;
- where you may expect audience responses to come, what those responses might be, and whether that is what you anticipated.

AFTER THE READING: DEBRIEFING

Assess the playwright's responses and your own: What did you learn? How are your responses to the material changed? Did this reading validate your early impressions of the script? What surprised you? What was confirmed? Do you need another reading with a different cast to clear up some unresolved issues? What do the actors have to say about what they did? What did they bring to the reading as interpreters of the characters and of the world of the play? Assess how the audience, if any, reacted during the reading; if you asked for their responses to specific questions, consider them.

After you assess all this information, meet privately with the playwright to compare your responses. Discuss at length what you both heard in the reading and what you gathered from the responses to it. Note qualities in the script that the actors missed on a first pass, but point out that, from a director's perspective, those things are in the script and will be revealed in rehearsals and performance. Often just hearing the script read tells the playwright what works, and/or gives him ideas for what needs to be done next. Consider whether your work on the script up to this point made it better. Is further development appropriate?

You may both agree that you do not wish to continue. Sometimes the playwright is appalled at the reading and wants to throw the script away; sometimes he is correct and you should both let the project drop. Sometimes the playwright is completely satisfied and sees no need to continue developing the script. Sometimes he is right; the script is ready for production. If you do not think so, say why and let the playwright decide.

Sometimes the playwright wants to continue the developmental process but you do not because you have done everything you can do with the script. In this case, suggest that the playwright pass the script on to another director. If you have suggestions for another director or institution, make them.

If you both wish to continue working on the script together, decide what to do next. This depends on what the playwright wants to accomplish. Ask what changes the playwright will make in the text as a direct result of the reading. What needs to be explored further in terms of your work as collaborators? Has the reading revealed areas that need further dramaturgy? Do you want to continue working with actors? Should you get different actors? Is it time to bring other contributors, such as designers, composers, or choreographers, into the process? Do you want to do a workshop, and if so what kind? Ask these questions as if you were working in an ideal world and then look to see what is practical. The practical considerations determine what comes next.

5 · REHEARSED
WORKSHOPS

> There are no rules about doing workshops, and there shouldn't be. The only valid question is: does the play need it?
>
> —Lloyd Richards, *Creating Theatre*

THE BEST METHOD of new script development is new play production. Any playwright, director, actor, designer, or audience member will prefer a full production to a workshop. Workshops are a means to that end, or at least they should be. Too often, workshops or other developmental "processes" are excuses to avoid the difficult and risky business of producing new plays. Consequently, there is a frequently cited backlash against play development workshops conducted without the prospect of future production, or workshopping a play unnecessarily so that it becomes "developed to death." However, properly conducted, the workshop can be a productive step in helping the playwright develop a new script. Once you move into the area of the workshop, you are beginning to explore the text, applying the conditions of rehearsal and performance. There are several kinds of workshops—each involves special techniques and each provides specific information about the script. The main categories of workshops are the *rehearsed reading*, the *minimally staged reading*, the *exploratory workshop*, and the full *workshop production*.

Whatever shape the workshop takes, playwright, director,

actors, and other collaborators use rehearsals, meetings, and possibly public presentations to explore in detail how the play works as an acted and directed text. The creative contributions of all the workshop participants reveal aspects of the script that only appear as the script comes to life in the theatre, where it belongs. You learn where it is theatrically effective and where you encounter difficulties making it work. You also begin to see how the script serves as a springboard for the creative contributions of director, actors, and other theatre artists. Where does the script open doors to further layers of meaning and where does it cause everyone to run into stone walls?

As in the earlier stages of development, ideally the playwright decides which form of workshop is the most useful and what if any changes to make in the text. While aspects of the writing itself are raised and addressed by all concerned, the playwright is the one who ultimately decides what to do about them. What the workshop provides is a final opportunity for the playwright to have complete control over his script before it goes into production. If the play needs a couple of hours of work and a few line changes to satisfy the playwright, that is what it gets. If it needs several months and major rewrites, then it gets the necessary time and work. Realistically, of course, your developmental work is also dictated by the practical circumstances of the workshop: the number of rehearsal hours you have, the speed at which everyone works, the available resources of talent and finances, and the pre-existing organizational constraints, like needing to fit into a curriculum or having to culminate in a public reading or performance.

The best developmental environment is one where you have unlimited access to the tools of the theatre, with no time or performance pressure and no institutional demands. Good luck.

Avoid falling into a particular developmental formula simply because it sounds good, because you have used it successfully before, or because "that's what they did with *Fences* and look how well that turned out!" You cannot predetermine the progress of a workshop. One of the fallacies of the institutional theatre is the notion that every play can be produced according to a uniform method. In development, especially, each play requires a custom-designed process that remains responsive throughout to the needs of the playwright and the material.

If you analyzed the script dramaturgically and heard it in an unrehearsed reading, you probably discovered avenues that need further exploration. By now you should have a good sense of the play's intention and how you anticipate its theatrical effects will operate. You may approach the workshop with specific questions you want to answer: Does the story make sense? Is the world of the play consistent? Are the play's issues integrated with its other elements? Does the event chain develop in a way that is theatrically compelling? Are the characters' words and actions actable? How do the play's patterns of language, ideas, and action interrelate to strengthen its intention? Further layers, complexities, and connections within the play begin to reveal themselves through extended rehearsal work. As you encounter these new aspects of the script, they guide your subsequent course.

In the workshop, you, the actors, and other collaborators explore these and similar questions and convey your discoveries and conclusions to the playwright, both through discussions and debriefings and through the writer's own rehearsal observations. The workshop lets the playwright see what happens when director, actors, and other collaborators work with the script: where it serves as an effective point of departure for their own creative work and where they struggle with the material.

Even at this early stage, the layered nature of developmental work becomes apparent. As you clarify major knots in the script, you can focus on the next more sophisticated level. Clearing up one problem often causes another problem to reveal both itself and its solution. This opening up of the script layer by layer continues throughout the developmental workshop and is one of the most exciting parts of developmental work.

Generally, you discover that some components of the script work very well. Confirmation of the play's strengths is an important part of the process; it provides anchor points for your further explorations. While you anticipated some of these strengths from developmental dramaturgy and the unrehearsed reading, you will discover new ones during the workshop that change your understanding of how the play works. Previously obscure aspects of the play now become apparent, perhaps creating a new understanding of how the play's elements operate, or revealing submerged issues that are more compelling than the play's overt messages.

As you work on the play you can also confidently expect to encounter problems—both anticipated and unanticipated. When you or the actors confront a problem in the material, first find ways to address it without asking for revisions. As you work through the problem, you may discover that the solution is, in fact, present in the script. If you cannot solve the problem working with the text as it stands, you may find you need to make an acting or directing addition that cannot be derived from the script, by providing, for example, an extratextual character motivation, a technical effect, or a piece of staging to make the scene work; or you may not be able to fix it without help from the playwright.

Always report the problems you encounter and what measures you take to the playwright. Let him in on your attempts at a solution. He may feel that you or the actors are mistaken in identifying some aspect of the script as a problem, because it clearly is deliberate and in line with his intention. He may remark that if you were a better director or had better actors it would work. He may be right.

It is more likely that the playwright will pay attention to your discoveries and find his own way to address the problem, either by incorporating the extratextual measures you suggest or going off, doing rewrites, and providing his own solution. Often just pointing out a problem you are unable to solve theatrically is sufficient to galvanize the playwright into rewrite action.[1]

If the playwright acknowledges the legitimacy of your struggles and wants assistance in addressing a problem in the text, there are several measures you can take without offering specific fixes or rewrites. The first and simplest approach is to discuss privately with the playwright what the glitch is specifically and why you or the actors are having difficulty. For example, he may have violated the script's internal logic, creating an incongruity; or the event chain may not be complete enough and the actor cannot justify the character's climactic action; or he may have set up a series of expectations and then not provided a pay-off; or the joke may simply not be funny. This kind of identification and analysis may be the key that unlocks the playwright's ability to solve this problem.

If the playwright is still stumped, there are several ways that you can use the process to help him. Offer him a panoply of possibilities, with the intention of stimulating his invention. Ask new questions, like "What if androids come in and take the baby?" Often the more outrageous the question the more freeing it is for the writer. If it is useful to the writer, set up improvisations with the actors: improvise the time the characters met; the time they punched each other. Have them act the subtext and not the dialogue, or dance the scene instead of speak it. The playwright may also "improvise" to unravel some knotty problem, writing the scene that is not in the play; writing the character's interior monologue; writing a separate character who knows everything and makes sapient remarks.

---

1. In fact, you need to guard against the playwright's attempting to solve every problem encountered in rehearsals by rewriting. The playwright's tendency is to say, "If there is a sin, it must be mine." Encourage the playwright to give you and the material a chance to work before making changes in the script.

The discovery of problems and how you all choose to address them are at the core of the developmental workshop. These discoveries will dictate the path of your work. This is where it gets strenuous. You disagree, you battle, you try a million things, you go up blind alleys, you get frustrated, and you often make great progress.

THE REHEARSAL PROCESS

A developmental rehearsal process differs from production oriented rehearsal processes because in development you are usually more interested in discovering what successive rehearsals reveal about the strengths and weaknesses of the script and conveying those discoveries to the playwright than you are in masking weaknesses and creating the best possible performance of the text. In development, director and actors work as explorers, theoretically free from the pressure to make things work at all costs for a paying audience and reviewers.

Sometimes the playwright will find it useful to be present at rehearsals, but not always. Often the fresh perspective that comes from days off will reveal new things to the playwright. He does not need to watch you grappling with the minutiae of the script, and sometimes it inhibits you or the actors to have the writer there. Often you and the actors may have to work in ways that might disturb the playwright. It is not uncommon to ask actors to do something wrong in order to get them to do something right.

Playwrights want the script to work all the time. Directors and actors must explore the material in ways that often make the script look and sound terrible. Send the writer off to the countryside for a couple of days and then show him the results of what you have done in his absence. Often the leaps in your work are more revealing than the tedious step-by-step progress. A little distance from the play gives the writer a clearer perspective on positive developments or nagging problems.

Phoning in Rehearsals. At least once during the developmental process, put the show together, and *phone in* a rehearsal. "Phoning in" a rehearsal is a technique designed to restore or retrieve your necessary objectivity. When you phone in a rehearsal, leave your script, clipboard, and pencil in your rehearsal bag. Let the rehearsal assistant start the rehearsal. Sit in the back of the room and just watch and listen. Do not make any notes, do not stop the rehearsal, do not make any pained noises. Pretend that you are sitting in on someone else's rehearsal. The first time you phone in a rehearsal can be as painful as the first time the producer sits in on your rehearsal: it induces complete paranoia and hypersensitivity. As you do it more, those sensations pass and you can actually see the show with some sort of objectivity.

THE REHEARSED READING

The *rehearsed reading* is a field test of your dramaturgy, with the added contributions of actors and any others involved in the process. The rehearsed reading is unstaged, functioning as table work that begins to give you a line-by-line analysis of the script. It does not provide much sense of how the script works theatrically; that knowledge comes when you put the show up on its feet. However, you begin to explore the event chain as action and to perceive the dynamics of the show—how it flows and builds—and what happens when actors begin to work on it, investigating character motivations, how they get from here to there, and how they interact.

Concentrate on the dynamic shape of the entire script by looking closely at the individual scenes, the connections between them, and their cumulative effect. Take the script apart to see how it works and then put it together again to see if it works.

Start by identifying each event and use your rehearsals to test the mechanics of each event and how each event works theatrically:

- First ask, what is it that makes this an event?
- How does this event affect the characters?
- How does this event convey the issues of the play?
- How does this event relate to the next event?
- Do the events conform to the logic of the play's story?

Expand your investigation from the individual events to the sequence of events that constitutes an entire scene or set of events. Ask the same questions, and begin to determine whether this scene has an organic cohesion:

- What are the patterns of the scene's shape and movement?
- Does it have rhythm, builds, and other dynamic attributes?
- How does it fit into the larger pattern of the play's events?
- Is it compelling?
- Does it add new information?
- Does it make sense in terms of the play's logic?

What the Actor Does

In the rehearsed reading the actors investigate how the characters function, what the relationships are, and whether each character has a playable set of individual characteristics. It is important to learn how much information the script gives the actors, not how much can be supplied out of directorial preconceptions. Encourage actors to look for complexity in motivation and characterization and play what they find, but not to add complexity unless they can support it from the script. Ask the actors to be scrupulous in reporting what they have to do to make the script work, particularly what they have to add. If they are confused, pay attention to their confusion; if they overlooked important information, point it out. Watch for frustration on the part of the actors; if they have trouble getting from A to Z it is likely that there are impediments to their doing so, perhaps gaps in the event chain, or missing pieces of character information.

The questions that actors raise in the developmental workshop are instrumental in letting the playwright see how the characters come to life in the theatre and how the characters work as roles to be performed. As the actors formulate and address these questions through their rehearsal work, they often illuminate the problems and provide approaches the playwright can implement.

THE MINIMALLY STAGED READING

The *minimally staged reading* provides a segue between the rehearsed reading and a workshop production. Sometimes a scene makes perfect sense as an idea but proves to be unintelligible when you physicalize it. Conversely, simply reading a scene from chairs will often not tell you what you need to know about how it works: the scene requires some form of staging or other nonverbal treatment. For example, the sound of chopping is as important a driving force as any of the dialogue in act 4 of *The Cherry Orchard*, and the silent shaving of Tilden's scalp in *Buried Child* is essential to the play's pattern of events. In the minimally staged workshop the focus shifts from the script on the page to the dynamics of what is happening moment-to-moment on the stage, providing a rough idea of how the script operates theatrically. You flag certain moments in the script—"This is where the big production number goes," for example: you are not actually staging the entire production number. It is as if you are hearing the score with only a piano accompaniment, although everyone knows that you will have a full orchestra in an actual production.

If the reading is presented to an audience, minimal staging creates an illusion of production, which makes it easier for them to respond to the work than to a rehearsed but unstaged reading.

It is valuable to have these indications of the full work, but this also presents the major pitfall of the minimally staged reading. Remember that the minimally staged reading is a hybrid form, useful insofar as it reveals something about the script that cannot be otherwise discovered. It is not an end in itself. Directors, accustomed to making things "work" on stage in performance, sometimes forget this caution and stage or rewrite the play to make their directing look good, or to try to make a "performance" out of what should be an exploratory exercise. This is another symptom of "workshopping a play to death."

Explore the dynamic shape of the script and characters as you do in the rehearsed reading. In addition, begin to investigate how the script works when the actors get up on their feet. The easiest way to do this is to use improvised staging by having the actors stand up. See what happens and where their impulses take them. A more complex approach is to start to apply directing by staging physical relationships and movement patterns. A puzzling moment may become clear when you physically isolate one character from the rest of the cast, for example.

If you choose to do formal staging, you can make a clear distinction between a minimally staged reading and a full production by creating a hybrid semi-staged reading: confine your staging only to those moments that absolutely require staging to be intelligible. *DO NOT* insert blocking to demonstrate your abilities as a director or to create a facsimile of a full production. This is the cardinal directorial rule of the developmental workshop and is surprisingly difficult for most directors to observe when they begin developmental work. Decide which physical actions are absolutely necessary for comprehension of the script. Pay attention to those stage directions that were read in the unrehearsed reading; these are probably the actions you need to stage. If the directions are complex (*they fight all over the set*), you may choose to set a tableau or sketch the action, while someone reads the complete stage direction. Do not waste your time with elaborate fights or choreography; flag or indicate the moment instead of realizing it fully.

If other theatrical effects are needed to forward the action, or are vital to establish the play's world, find a way to indicate them. Sometimes, announcing their existence is sufficient: "*as the play progresses, the walls of the set move in to trap the actors in an ever-smaller playing space.*"

Lay out the simplest possible floor plan. Use rehearsal furniture. Do not include anything just for the sake of pretty pictures; do not include anything decorative; do not include anything that is not absolutely necessary for the action.

Consultation with designers can be helpful in clarifying the script's nonverbal language. A set model, a costume sketch, an idea for a lighting or sound effect can help everyone involved understand how a particular moment or aspect of the script works. You will probably not use these design elements in the minimally staged reading, but designer's approaches to the material can be helpful at this point, contributing to your understanding of how the script operates in three dimensions.

Unless there is a good reason to memorize lines for a particular scene, actors continue to work with scripts in hand. This ensures that they remain open to script changes. Of course, it may be necessary for actors to memorize lines in a particular section of the script in order to execute vital staging.

THE EXPLORATORY WORKSHOP

The *exploratory workshop*, in our usage, is completely process oriented. You are not working to satisfy an audience; usually there is no presentation element at all. The focus is on exploring or playing with the material. Sundance Institute Playwrights Laboratory, for example, asks the playwrights what they want to do and provides resources as requested. A playwright may want five dancers, or opera singers. He may want the actors to hang out in the Greyhound terminal and bring back characters. He may want to do the script on the beach, or backwards. In this situation, the theatre is truly serving as a laboratory where playwrights are free to explore their material.

The exploratory workshop is not necessarily confined to investigating how the script works as performance but rather plays with the material in ways that the playwright thinks may help the writing. Some playwrights, like Caryl Churchill, begin the writing process this way, using the actors in the workshop to generate ideas. Then the writer goes off with a briefcase full of notes and comes back sometime later with a draft script ready for further development.

Explorations may involve experimenting with different actors in the roles, radical restructuring of the script's event chain, incorporating the use of other production elements like lighting, sound, masks, or dance, experimenting with different performance venues, and anything else that offers the playwright and the script creative momentum. These types of exploratory procedures can be used throughout the developmental process, if you have the time and inclination.

THE WORKSHOP PRODUCTION

A workshop production allows a script to breathe on its own without the sometimes awkward compromises of a minimally staged reading. In a workshop production you mount the play with minimal production support, focusing attention on what is happening in the script rather than on completed design or marketing choices.

You move into a more collaborative phase of development by applying the director's and actors' rehearsal processes to the script. Actors and director begin to work independently of the playwright on their own areas of competence.

Organize rehearsals the same way you would work on a finished script, with two important differences: you do not have the pressures of a full production process, with its attendant distractions of design meetings, technical rehearsals, opening nights, critics, and paying audiences; and you do not use directing and acting solutions to cover up problems in the script. Instead, your work should show the playwright what he has and let him decide what to do about it.

Typically, the workshop production will encompass all the phases of previously discussed developmental work, starting with dramaturgy and moving through an unrehearsed reading and a rehearsed reading into full staging with minimal props, costumes, sets, lights, and technical effects.

Rehearsal work may stimulate the playwright to explore new material, different interpretations, or staging, for example. Always try out what the playwright suggests. Potential solutions to problems you identify may come from many different sources and may produce disagreements. Fight for your ideas and the good ideas of other collaborators, but let the playwright win and continue to guide the process toward the refinement of his play, not yours.

WORKING WITH THE PLAYWRIGHT

Throughout whatever developmental process you undertake, continue to work collaboratively with the playwright, using the rehearsal discoveries to guide your mutual explorations of the script. An important part of the workshop process is translating actors', designers' and director's responses to the piece into language that the playwright can use, according to the vocabulary you established previously. If an actor turns around in rehearsal and screams, "I don't know what I'm doing here," you may need to present this dilemma to the playwright as a question about the character's event chain. If a designer keeps coming in with sketches of abstract shapes as a response to a script that calls for realism, this is a world-of-the-play question for the playwright. If, as a director, you are struggling to make that third confrontation scene in a row different from the previous two, explore this privately with the playwright as a question concerning the pattern of events.

Convey to the playwright what you are doing directorially with the script. When you direct the piece it becomes more dimensional and your earlier understandings of it sometimes change radically. Like the actors, you will find that there are places where you struggle to make things work or where the play stimulates your own creative impulses. When you begin to direct, you may finally understand how a specific moment works theatrically, so that you can sit down with the playwright and say, "Look, this is the climax of the scene right here, and it works!" This either means, "Good for you, you wrote it right," or "We don't really need this other dialogue to explain what's going on, because the moment's already there."

Discuss how rewrites and cuts work in rehearsal and where additional rewrites may be necessary. Pass on actors' comments and questions. Note where they are struggling, where they are finding things that you have not previously identified that help clarify the script.

UGLYVILLE

At some stage in every creative process, and especially in the developmental process, you, your playwright, and your cast will hit Uglyville.[2] Uglyville is the place where your judgment departs, you lose sight of everything, you do not like your work, the script, or the actors, and there is no health in anything. It can and does happen any time, although the most

---

2. A term coined by the Overtone Theatre, San Francisco.

common time is about two-thirds of the way through the process, when you are committed to an approach and have inevitably lost some of your initial flexibility. This is a normal phase; you can get through it if you do your preliminary work carefully and clearly and make notes as you go along. Keep on with your original intentions even if they seem invalid to you at the moment. This may be the time to ask the playwright to absent himself from rehearsals a while. It is particularly important not to panic and start flailing around, making changes and acting erratically in a desperate attempt to get out of Uglyville. Take solace in the fact that this, too, shall pass.

WORKING WITH THE AUDIENCE

As part of the developmental process it may be useful to assess the experience that the play creates by presenting it for an audience. Ultimately, the script, and your work on it, is not a creation in a vacuum or even the hothouse of the rehearsal hall. Its full intention is only realized when it intersects with and influences an audience. You can usefully gauge the experience of the play for an audience by controlling the kind of audience you have and by guiding the post-performance response you allow. As with the other phases of development, the playwright should decide what kinds of audience and response, if any, are the most helpful.

Be aware of the vulnerability that every writer feels about putting work up for public scrutiny, especially work in progress. Many playwrights correctly detest this process, regarding it as a kind of public humiliation imposed on them and their work to serve some other institutional priority such as giving subscribers the illusion of involvement in the creative process, or satisfying grant givers that the theatre is developing new works, or convincing a marketing department or board of directors that a play will sell. Avoid these situations, and focus on a positive use of the audience as genuine collaborators. Protect the work from potential abuses and try to develop audiences, and uses of them, that aid your understanding of where the script works and where it does not.

Types of Audiences

You can use a panel of experts, an invited audience, or a general audience. You get different sorts of responses from each.

Arguably, the most sophisticated and technical response comes from a *panel of experts*. New Dramatists in New York often asks three or four respondents to comment on the script, usually a day or two after the presentation and in private. Playwright, director, and dramaturg, if any, are present at these sessions. The respondents may be other playwright members of New Dramatists, or others whose opinion is respected by the primary participants. In other new script development situations, an outside adjudicator, dramaturg, or festival critic responds. Respondents' biases are usually either overtly stated or obvious in their comments. Responses are sophisticated and technical, typically addressing story, event chain, dynamics, characterization, issues, language, and images.

These responses are valuable insofar as they help the playwright and other collaborators understand the effect of their work on an audience member who knows something about the theatre and who is able to articulate those responses clearly with specific references to the way(s) the play creates its meanings. There is a danger that a panel of experts will override the script's intention and impose their own priorities or even begin to suggest specific fixes. Do not allow anyone, no matter how illustrious or articulate, to rewrite the play or force it into a conception that is not consistent with the playwright's intention.

You will get less-focused but still "informed" responses from an *invited audience* composed of people accustomed to hearing new plays read. The members of a playwrights' conference or new play reading series constitute this type of audience. They are familiar with the general bases of the developmental process and can respond specifically and technically to the work.

Invited audiences can be useful in responding to specific questions. This kind of audience sometimes includes people who want to give advice about how the playwright should solve specific problems or how the respondent would solve these problems. These kinds of remarks should be carefully monitored by the moderator, who should firmly refocus the discussion of noncorrective responses to the script.

People who work with new material are in almost unanimous agreement that the *general audience* or "wild" audience is the least helpful in its post-performance comments on a play in progress. On the other hand, if a post-performance discussion is avoided, the general audience, especially when it is not heavily weighted with friends and relatives, may be the most helpful in assessing performance response to the script. By sitting in the house with them as they experience the play you can learn which things work, where attention flags, where their emotions are engaged, and where they breathe with the actors. None of these responses suggest specific fixes, but they are valuable in telling you and the writer whether the play creates the experience that you want it to.

Types of Response

Besides controlling the composition of the audience, you can also control the kinds of response you allow, first by how you prepare the audience, and second by how you conduct the response session itself.

Decide beforehand whether the playwright will be present at the response and, if he chooses to be present, whether he will be identified as the playwright. If he is identified, does the writer wish to sit in the audience itself or in front of the audience? Some playwrights prefer to be present but unidentified, believing that this allows the audience to respond more freely. Conducting the response session with the playwright in front of the audience often means that the playwright will not be able to hear the response, usually because he is on the spot. If the audience response is unfavorable, the playwright is in a particularly awkward position.

After deciding together whether the playwright is present and/or identified at the response session, decide what type of audience response to solicit. Different kinds of responses elicit different information from the audience.

No Post-show Discussion. You may choose not to ask the audience to speak to the play at all. This is probably the most productive use of a general audience. When you choose this option be sure that during the reading you keep your attention closely focused on the audience and their reactions to the piece, because you derive your information from watching and listening to how they respond. You learn:

- where attention flags;
- where they are confused;
- where it works;
- where they think it is funny.

Open Response. An open response is the closest you get to a free-for-all. During an open response you allow the audience to engage in an unmoderated discussion of the play. Many developmental directors and playwrights find this the least helpful kind of response. With a general audience you hear a lot of literary criticism. Often the audience wants to rewrite the play or at least to tell the playwright how it should be written. Sometimes these responses can be devastating, particularly when an audience member responds negatively to an actor or an issue in the script. These discussions often bog down with insignificant details or mundane generalities.

Controlled Response. Most directors feel that audience response is most useful when a moderator controls the response, usually by asking specific questions about the script and about the audience's reaction to it. In a controlled response situation it is wise to prepare the audience by explaining to them what you want from them. You may wish to explicitly place some areas out of bounds: for instance, you may say, "We are very interested in your answers to some specific questions [and name them], but we are going to ask you not to engage in corrective criticism—that is, don't tell the playwright how you would have written the play or what you would do to fix it."

The questions you pose to the audience are usually questions of fact: Do they understand the progression of the events or are certain pivotal moments confusing to them? Was the incident of the letter clear? Did they understand that Janice was Howard's daughter, abandoned at birth? Did they realize the world of the play was post-nuclear-holocaust? What questions are they left with? You may be less than satisfied with a scene or a character: the audience can tell you whether they share your misgivings.

Determine in advance what the playwright wants to know, and you may suggest additional questions you wish to ask. Do not expect the audience to function as a corporate dramaturg; use the audience for *your* purposes. It may be that all you want the audience to do is provide encouragement as a means of keeping the playwright writing without inhibition. "Only tell me what you loved" is a perfectly appropriate request of an audience response session.

In the best response circumstances a moderator should ensure the following ground rules:

- no corrective criticism;
- playwright should not defend or justify the work to the audience;
- playwright should not interpret the work for the audience;
- questions asked of the writer should be turned back as questions to other audience members; see if someone in the audience got it or how the audience disagrees on certain points rather than having the playwright provide "the answer."

Thank the audience for their response. Remember, they are not stupid. It is not useful to take the attitude that if the audience were smart enough they would understand what you are trying to do. It is significant that they did not get it, and you should at least consider their confusion and determine what caused it.

Taking Critiques

Often it is difficult to listen to audience remarks and not respond or defend the work or the collaborators. If you enter into a dialogue with the audience you run the risk of not hearing the important things they say because you are busy trying to tell them what they missed. To prevent this, and to keep yourself busy while you listen, write down everything everyone says, nod a lot, and make interesting and interested noises. Then, later, when you no longer have the applause in your ears, or when you have achieved a little distance on your disappointment that they did not fall at your feet and throw roses at you, you can go over your notes, first alone, and then with the playwright, and figure out what they really said.

Whether and How to Incorporate Audience Comments

If there is more than one presentation, especially with a day or two between performances, you may incorporate relatively minor rewrites based on audience response (especially if those responses indicate confusion) before the next performance. Then you can test the rewrites on the next audience. If the audience responses confirm that major rewrites are in order, you probably will wait until after all the performances, when the dust has settled, so you can evaluate things with a clearer head.

There is always the danger of trying to please everyone in the audience. Be sure that you continue to encourage the playwright to maintain the integrity of the piece and not to try to please everyone. It is not uncommon for scripts to be rewritten to death, based on audience comments. Remember that you are working to realize the script's intention, not trying to please a panel of Neilson families.

AFTER THE RUN

After the final performance, have a summarizing meeting, where you and the playwright discuss the gist of the audience remarks. Sometimes there is a clear consensus that the playwright's intentions are not being transmitted to the audience. Sometimes the playwright is saying the opposite of what he thinks. Sometimes characters do not function as intended. Sometimes the audience as a whole will not understand the story or the event chain. These are serious matters and should be discussed with cool heads and a little distance. Alternatively, some things may have worked very well and conformed entirely to the playwright's intention. Leave these things alone and resist the temptation to tamper with them. Consider as well the comments of actors and other collaborators on the production. What did performing the material add to their understandings of the script?

CHOOSING WHAT TO DO NEXT

At the end of whatever developmental process you chose, meet with the playwright to summarize what you accomplished together and to explore what to do next. The playwright will probably have one of three responses: (1) produce it; (2) work on it some more, either with you or someone else; or (3) abandon it. Explore the playwright's reasons for responding as he does. Then offer him your honest evaluation of the script, always qualifying your opinions with the idea that they represent *your* response and not *the* response. You may believe that the project should be abandoned. You may suggest that the work needs further development with you or with someone else who can bring something to it that you cannot. You may believe that the script is ready for a full production and work with the playwright to secure that production.

Whatever you decide, take the time to assess this particular experience carefully. You and the actors have inevitably imprinted your work and sensibilities on the play. It may well be that your collaboration helped make the play more effective. At the very least, the writer participated in moving the script from the study into the world of the theatre, where it belongs.

APPENDIX: INTERVIEWS

RECOMMENDED READING

INDEX

APPENDIX:

INTERVIEWS

THE FOLLOWING interviews, conducted over a several-year period with some of the country's leading participants in new script development, reinforce many of the approaches presented in *Scriptwork* from the perspectives of theatre professionals whose daily lives and work involve the productive interaction of playwrights and directors. The interviewees, however, do not speak with a single voice, and the differences in their approaches and vocabularies offer a useful corrective to the notion that there is a distinct method of new script development that always works. What does emerge from these readings is the central principle that playwrights can and do benefit from working with directors who use theatrical exploration of the script as a nurturing process, applying the tools and sensibilities of stage performance with vigilant respect for the writer's ownership of the play.

ALMA BECKER

Alma Becker is a director and teacher. As Artist in Residence in the Department of Theatre at Skidmore College in New York she has directed *Red Noses*, *The House of Bernarda Alba*, and the premiere of Dana Foley's *The Mudwoman*. She has directed premiere productions: *Night Luster* and *Free Fall* by Laura Harrington, *Old Black Joe* and *A Hopeful Interview with Satan* by OyamO, *Surrender/A Flirtation* by Dana Foley, *Primary Colors* by Steve Carter, *Beirut* by Alan Bowne, and *God's Little Helper* by Steve Coates. Other productions she has directed include *Retribution Rag* by Buffy Sedlachek, *Giant on the Ceiling* by Alice Eve Cohen, *Master Harold and the Boys*, *Landscape of the Body*, *Fefu and Her Friends*, *A Moon for the Misbegotten*, and *A Taste of Honey*. In New York she has directed for Theater for the New City, The Womens Project and Productions, Primary Stages, and West Bank Cafe Downstairs Theatre Bar. Regionally she has worked in New Jersey, Maine, Minneapolis, Wisconsin, California, Iowa, and Virginia. In addition, Becker has had long associations with several writer's organizations: the Playwrights Center and Midwest Playlabs in Minnesota, Bay Area Playwrights Festival in San Francisco, and New Dramatists in New York, where she was an NEA Directing Fellow and later Director in Residence on a Jerome Foundation grant. She is also director of her own group, The Island Company.

Becker has worked with many writers on readings and developmental workshops, including, Daniel Thierrault, August Baker, Laura Censabella, Sherry Kramer, Phil Bosakowski, Jeff Jones, Gilbert Girion, Mac Wellman, Connie Congdon, Bennet Cohen, Julie Jensen, and Gordon Stanley. At Theatre of the First Amendment, at George Mason University, she recently worked with OyamO on an updated version of *One Third of a Nation*, a living newspaper on homelessness. She has also directed *Faces: A Living Newspaper on Aids* by Carolyn Anderson and Wilma Hall in Virginia and upstate New York. In the summer of 1990 Becker worked with theatre artists in Nairobi, Kenya, developing a play on the subject of sex education to tour schools. She is currently collaborating on a book for young directors.

WHEN I WORK with a writer, I say, "Please listen very carefully to the questions that I put to you right at the beginning. That's probably the most helpful conversation we'll have." The director/playwright question session lays the groundwork for the collaboration. I consider myself a kind of audience, a keen observer, and I think that's one of the things I can do for playwrights. So, based on my experience, my knowledge, my intuition, my instinct, I frame the questions that I feel are going to have the greatest impact on the work, possibly things that the writer has not thought of, or that I feel the writer is working toward but hasn't achieved, something that's under the writing that might need to come up and be focused on.

My first question for the playwright is always, "What is your impulse for writing the play?" I listen carefully to the answer. The answer might be an image, a metaphor, a story, a personal experience, a theme, a character, and so on, but in whatever form the writer responds, I begin to get a sense of where they have been true to the impulse and where they've strayed from it.

The questions are specific to each play. My approach to each play changes, based on the style of that play. The play dictates the response. Generally, I try to understand the logic of the play; I want to know that what I perceive from the play is what is intended by the writer, and if it's not, then why not.

Based on a number of readings I give my perceptions and visceral response to the play. These comments usually address story, characters, structure, and style, among others, and include the strengths and possible weaknesses of the play.

This scenario is based on the assumption that the playwrights feel they need the developmental process and can benefit from it. Some playwrights are eager for director and actor input, others simply need to hear the play aloud in order to continue to work on it. It usually depends on where the writer is in her or his process.

The director is a sounding board for the playwright. If you are attuned to the playwright and the world she or he is creating you start "seeing" from their perspective, you feel their intentions. For me that is a true collaboration.

Directors who come in and say, "Okay, I want you to do this and this and this, because this will make this better," can overwhelm a playwright and get in the way of the writer doing her or his work. The playwright is the playwright, the director is not the playwright.

I like to set up goals with a writer for the workshop process.

I structure the workshop around the goals, with room for change based on our discoveries during the process. We might say, "Let's follow the throughline of this character. This is the main character in the play, and seems to be the least interesting. Why is that? Where does this character not work?" And we'll focus on that and explore it.

"Play development" can mean many things: reading with no rehearsal, reading with rehearsal, reading with or without an audience, reading with or without actor input, staged reading, sit-down reading, round table reading, or combinations of these. The process may last hours or weeks.

I think a cold reading with good actors can serve a playwright as well as a longer workshop. It depends on the needs of the playwright. The actors in a reading or workshop are crucial to the success of the workshop. In readings we seem to ask the actors to speed up the process: to make choices that will serve the play without the rehearsal process behind them. I look for actors who are flexible and willing to work fast and dirty. I encourage actors to play together, to work off each other. I express the goals of the workshop to trigger participation and to guide the actors.

As I listen to the play I sometimes follow along in my script, making notes as the reading progresses, particularly when one of our goals is editing.

Movement in readings can be useful. I like readings with some movement. It can be as simple as telling the actors "there's a door left and a door right, and a table with five chairs. Just come in and use the chairs whenever you need to." I have a technique when I want to go further than that: I create rough blocking prior to the rehearsal and come in and give the actors the basic moves, having them write in their scripts. This step usually follows several sessions of reading and discussion.

Murray Schisgal said some years ago at a conference at New Dramatists, "What is this reading stuff? Theatre is not for reading. Theatre is for watching." I had to agree with him that day. It can be frustrating to put the whole burden of theatricality on the words, especially when so many of our playwrights are working with a strong visual sense integrated into the text.

I go through phases of liking staged readings and not. If they overwhelm the text, then I dislike them. If the focus stays with the text, then they're fine.

Sometimes we want to test something about the play. I did one workshop that was very physical, with action happening in four or more places on the stage, a page of dialogue in one place, a page in the next, a page in the next. We said, "Let's find out if this is physically possible." We devoted two afternoons to staging the first act of the play. We discovered it *did* work, which was a direct benefit for the playwright. She relaxed, said, "Okay, that's fine," and kept going, rather than waiting for a production to find out.

Some playwrights are active participants in discussion and rehearsals during the developmental workshop. Others are observers and note takers. I encourage discussion between actors and playwright. I'm thinking of a specific instance recently that was one of those prize situations. We had a reading of the play with a group of actors; we got their questions or observations—things like, "Why is this character always complaining?" So you write all those things down whether you agree with them or not. Then there was a three or four day break when I spoke with the writer; she rewrote; we got the same group of actors, because we liked them very much. We came back and reread the new draft of the script; new feedback, more time. The playwright had taken very large steps with the script before we started working on our feet for a staged reading. The actors also had this rehearsal time, time to study the characters, to see where the character was when the process began and how the character developed in the new draft. They could see their influence on the play.

As more plays are developed and fewer plays are produced, I have seen a maturing of playwrights involved in the developmental process. I feel they are more selective about how and when they allow their work to be developed. Sometimes development can feel like a factory and the playwright gets swallowed up by the machinery.

LEE BLESSING

Lee Blessing is the author of *A Walk in the Woods*, which opened on Broadway in 1988. The play was nominated for the Pulitzer, the Tony Award, and the Olivier Award in London's West End, where it starred Sir Alec Guinness. It has since been seen in productions worldwide and on PBS's *American Playhouse*. Other plays by Blessing include *Fortinbras*, *Two Rooms*, and *Down the Road*, all commissioned and produced by Des McAnuff at the La Jolla Playhouse; *Cobb*, given its world premiere by Lloyd Richards at the Yale Repertory Theatre; *Eleemosynary*, produced by the Manhattan Theatre Club; and *Riches*, *Independence*, *Oldtimer's Game*, and *Nice People Dancing to Good Country Music*, all originally produced by the Actors Theatre of Louisville. Blessing's latest play, *Lake Street Extension*, was directed by Jeanne Blake in its world premiere at Ensemble Theatre of Cincinnati.

Blessing has developed works at the O'Neill National Playwrights Conference, the Sundance Institute, New Dramatists in New York, and the Playwrights Center in Minneapolis. He has received grants from the National Endowment for the Arts and the Guggenheim, Bush, McNight, and Jerome Foundations. His original screenplay, *Cooperstown*, starring Alan Arkin and Graham Green, aired on the TNT network.

I'VE WORKED in workshops, in nonperformance workshops, cold readings, sit-down readings, staged readings. At the Playwrights Center in Minneapolis, I've done all of those things. At the O'Neill we had staged readings. I became a member of New Dramatists in New York in 1985, and I've done work there similar to the work I've done at the Playwrights' Center. At Louisville it was a matter of them selecting a script and jumping immediately into production, with some revision. At La Jolla Playhouse it was a matter of doing two plays on commission where I worked very late right up to the brink of performance on essentially first-draft plays—plays that I personally had taken through a couple of drafts but that were first drafts in terms of audience. I've worked a lot of different ways with a lot of different people.

When I have worked with people that ultimately I've clicked with, a number of different approaches can work. Various scripts lend themselves to various approaches, too. Some scripts develop very quickly; they get a sense of themselves almost immediately, and others are very slow to formulate what they want to say. Certain scripts have been better served by pretty quick processes, and other scripts have been better served by going very slowly.

I think everybody wishes he had a secret formula for determining which directors he's going to be able to work with and which ones he can't. It's hard to say how a director is going to do on a particular play just because you've seen an earlier production. I've had an experience where a director directed one of my plays wonderfully and turned around and did a different play on a totally different subject terribly. So that can happen, because the director knew the one world but didn't know the other. It's important to know what your director's strengths and weaknesses are, because nobody can direct all plays well, just as nobody can write all plays well. It's rare, but you can run into a situation where they just don't have a clue.

It's a little like dating, and everybody has personality types that they respond to more readily than others. I've always enjoyed working with directors who have a lot of energy. I find myself attracted to that. I'm not sure it's always good. I've had some energetic directors who did not necessarily interpret the play well. On a very subjective level, I get nervous if the director doesn't seem to have time to talk to me, or is too busy with other things. If I don't feel like I'm a major priority with a director, that's a difficult situation, one I'm not sure I need to be in.

I'm sure that directors have their own ideas about playwrights too. It's not a one-way street. Some playwrights get a lot more paranoid than they need to, or are much more controlling than they need to be, too.

I want to feel as if there are not a whole lot of games being played, that the director doesn't have a whole set of agendas that are in conflict with mine, or that the director is ignoring my priorities. As closely as I can align my priorities with the director's, that's how happy I'm going to be working with him or her. Fundamentally, I like to feel that there's a loyalty to the project, that the person is there because they're excited about that play, and their interpretation and mine are closely matched. There's nothing more important than getting the play interpreted correctly. It's more important than any other decision or series of decisions that a director has to make. I don't think it's possible unless the director has an honest rapport with the playwright and really understands the play. If he doesn't there's going to be a lot of trouble. Also I think it's important not to powertrip a lot, as far as who's doing the casting, who's hiring whom, who's looking the brightest in rehearsal, that sort of thing. If you get into those kinds of contests, then you're probably working with the wrong person.

I have had situations where I've worked on premiere productions with directors who did not understand the play, but were good at buffaloing me, getting me to worry about things that were incidental, and have me constantly rewriting those when I should have been there objecting to the major mistakes that were going on.

If you're in a situation where a director is much more experienced than you, that can sometimes translate into a big problem. When it's early in your career, you don't have very much purchase with artistic directors and producers. You can't simply walk in and say, "We've got to replace somebody." So you can sometimes end up stuck with a production you don't like.

I feel, looking back on it, that there are times when I should have pulled the script, that there are productions I should have said "No" to, even in rehearsal, and I would have been better off. But I think I've been fortunate as time has gone on to be able to identify people that that's not going to happen with.

One thing I've definitely learned about being a playwright in this kind of relationship with producers and directors is that the decisions that you make early are really the only decisions you have. The longer you go into the production process, the harder it is to affect anybody, including the director. Ultimately the process is one where you have the property, and slowly the control of that property is taken over by the director and ultimately by the actors. By opening night there's almost nothing you or the director can do—except hope you've made good decisions.

Once a director and I achieve a level of trust, then it's really a question of what sorts of stylistic decisions and detail work we are going to do together now that we feel that we understand what is the right road for this play. That's really the crucial set of decisions.

All three of the people who I've been working with lately have the capacity to put into a nutshell—to find the kernel of—what is the matter or what is missing or what isn't working or what is a little skewed in the script, and come back to me and say "This is fine, but are we passing over something here that we should be dealing with? Is there a key phrase that somebody should be uttering about this sort of thing? Is this an honest emotional response at this point in the play?" Throughout my career the directors who I've enjoyed working with most usually had the capacity to do the hard dramaturgical work, as well as direct.

At the Playwrights Center usually I will do a workshop in three or four days with actors. There are some playwrights who use the rehearsal period much more aggressively than I do. Some playwrights like to write in rehearsal, they really like to improvise a lot and work with actors, but I don't. I'm just not comfortable doing that, never have been. Mostly I like to sit down and listen to what I've written being read and then have some breaks to talk to the actors about what's not working for them.

The actors are usually generous about responding. They usually don't have a big overview about what they've just done, but they've read a role, and they often have strong feelings about "Why didn't I do this? Why did I do that? Am I really justified in doing this? Am I really supposed to like this person or what?" They can ask some very telling questions.

Then we'll do a sit-down reading so I can get an audience's response. It's really helpful for me to hear audiences' responses. At the Center we always have a period of comments and questions after the reading, from whoever's come to listen. They'll often raise some interesting points, but fundamentally I'm there to sit behind them all and watch them and listen to their response during the reading, because really in any play the fundamental thing that the playwright is concerned with is what's happening in the audience, what's happening *to* people who are listening and watching the play. You can tell if they're rapt or not, if they're involved and compelled by what's going on. It may not tell you *why*, but you'll certainly be able to pinpoint much better what's working and what's not.

There is certainly the whole catalog of useless remarks that everybody always hears. It's not really that they seem so useless to an objective observer, but playwrights are very subjective beasts, especially when you're talking about something they've been working on myopically for the last few months. Someone else could understand and deal with it, but the playwright feels like he's hearing a foreign language. For the most part, I respond to audience comments just the way I respond to written reviews. What I look for in either of those things is an openness of spirit and a desire to find out what's working and explore why more of it isn't.

When things are positively couched, it makes a lot more sense to a playwright than when they're negatively couched. Unfortunately critics are journalistic beasts rather than theatrical ones, and for that reason they have a whole set of different priorities. One of those is to be confrontational. Confrontational commentary is something that I can rarely use to turn around and improve a play. It isn't that there isn't something to be gained from being attacked now and then and having to fundamentally question whether this is even how you should be doing it, but for the most part I find that when people start out with what's working for them and then have questions about what isn't, that's a lot more useful.

Usually, after a reading or workshop, I need to go away from the script for a while, to put it down. I make the notes that I need to make—of responses after a reading or what the actors have said during a workshop—then I'll wait a week or two or even longer before I go back and work on the play. That usually helps me boil down what is most important. A lot of the craft of playwriting is being able to focus on what's most important and letting everything else depend on that.

I have the feeling that I'm lucky to be working as a playwright in this era, when there are a number of formal structures set up specifically to foster play development. It's a great way to meet and work with directors *before* getting involved with them in a high-stakes production.

PHIL BOSAKOWSKI

Phil Bosakowski's plays include *Chopin in Space, Wheel and Deal, Buster Comes Through,* and *Nixon Apologizes to the Nation.* They have been performed in New York and various regional theatres, including Yale Rep, Denver Theatre Center, and the Bay Area Playwrights Festival. He has received fellowships from the National Endowment for the

Arts and was recently awarded the Bodkin Prize for *How I Got My Apartment*, a film script developed at the National Playwrights Conference in Waterford, Connecticut. He served as director of the Playwrights Workshop at the University of Iowa and taught playwriting at Dartmouth College and Princeton University.

I'VE WORKED in situations where I've come in with a play and I've had either a staged reading or an informal sit-down reading, where it was totally geared towards me. I've also worked in situations where an artistic director and a dramaturg and kind of a board of directors already had a plan about what they wanted and commissioned me to do a new work, and I guess everything in between.

The best is where you sit down with actors who you trust and a director who you trust and just find out what's in the script. I've worked with women directors and men and I have a tendency to appreciate working with women directors early on, because in general, the women directors I've worked with have all said, "Well, what is it you have here, and how can we help you see your vision?" So I find—and I hate to use this term—that midwifing the play is often in better hands when it's in female hands. It seems that most women directors tend to have female talents that help them realize the work. They keep the ball in your court in a very positive and generous way.

A wise film writer said, "It's never as good as the moment you're sitting there by yourself and you put it down on paper." From that point on, any smart playwright realizes it's a process of giving up authority and vision. But you hope to get it to the point so that your interpreters have an easier time of it, so they can interpret rather than have to invent.

Another thing that I'm always aware of with myself is that, like most Americans, if I hear a stronger voice than my own I'll say, "Yea, that's right." I have a tendency to give up authority a little early in a show, I think. Sometimes we may be going down the wrong direction, where I just find myself compromising a vision. What I try to do now as an antidote to that is whenever I go into any rehearsal, whether it's a rehearsal for a staged reading or a cold reading I try to write down exactly what it is I'm looking to do in this process, so that I have something I can always go back to, even if it gets abandoned.

My plays tend to have a lot of loose strings, so the developmental process is one of either connecting the dots, or tying the strings that are there, or building bridges from one image to another, from one scene to another. A good collaborative process is when somebody helps me find the ones that are worth tying or connecting without adding new ones.

Directing to me is one of the most ephemeral things and what I'm always looking for with directors is someone who can communicate. The very best directors are great audiences, and the good directors that I've worked with are very responsive, not only to what I'm giving them, but to what the actors give them, or to what a designer gives them. I guess the first thing I look for is someone who's a ready audience for what I've got, and then watch them as they chat with me or talk about designers in terms of their ability to verbally articulate their vision.

Deciding whether I can work with a particular director is almost an intuitive process. I can think of one director—I was desperately looking for a director, the production was set up, and I didn't have a director yet, and gave the script to a guy, and he wanted to get together the next night and talk about it. And he had gone through it, you could tell. He had knocked out every beat in the play, including the beats that were in the stage directions, and he had just done the whole play. I thought, "This guy really wants to do it." The first thing out of his mouth was, "I love this play, even if I don't get to direct it." That's always a nice thing to have them say.

If they start fixing the play before they identify it, that scares me. Later on in the rehearsal process when you're going to be showing this to the public and you have the sense that

"We've gotta make this work, why don't you do that?" I think there's a time for that, but I think even through the first production you want to get as much of your vision out as possible without its filtering through other people.

Once a play has been done maybe twice, it's fair game. You can even deconstruct it if you want. But when you're working with that first time through, you want to nurse that little thing along. I understand the impulse to make things work, but with new work especially, you do it because you don't know if it's going to work.

You try to start small, I think that's the smart way to do it. You get a couple of your friends to sit around and you have them read it and you just let it build. I would never open a play in New York again, I think that's really stupid.

What I do is I just sit there and pretend I'm listening. I don't follow the text on the page or anything. I just sit there like an audience member and try to listen to it. I've found when I'm listening to a scene and thinking, "Well, as soon as they get through this scene, it'll be okay again," then the red flag goes up that there's something not working there. You listen to the rhythms of the actors, when they seem to be skating real well, when there seems to be a music or rhythm in the character, then I know we're okay. But it's amazing how quiet the room gets when the scene isn't working. There's something—there's a rush of air or something when a scene is working, and there's an edge that I can't quite put my finger on; but it just goes right out the window when the thing stops working. You can really feel when a play is working. A friend of mine says that there are two kinds of plays, the kind that gives energy to you and the kind that takes energy from you. I'm so sensitive to when one of my plays is sponging up energy instead of giving it.

At the O'Neill [Theatre Center's National Playwrights Conference] they invite everybody up for four days and we each have to read our own play by ourselves to all the other writers and the directors and to whoever else is there. You find out a lot about your play that way. You find out what's unspeakable, what's unplayable; usually you're sort of at a panic level where you can't do much more than just blah-blah-blah the words. I tried to perform mine when I did it, with a pen in hand, and when the thing died I put check marks in the margin. We were sitting in sort of a big living room with a fireplace right behind you and a huge oil painting of Eugene O'Neill, and you kind of swear that every once in a while his eyes start fluttering too at some of the slow moments. I actually physically noticed that when the play was working—people are sitting in chairs or sofas and some are on the floor—they actually start getting closer to you. They're with it, and they get closer. When the thing stops working, they just start moving away physically. It was just amazing.

I find that during rehearsals it's useful to just go away for a couple of days. You really have to pick your spots. Sometimes it's useful to be around for a couple of days to answer the dumb questions like who's related to whom, and where is Buster while Douglas is talking. That's fine, but then I think you have to let your collaborators be silly for a couple of days. Rehearsal is a time to make big mistakes, and a lot of actors and directors are a little chary about having the playwright there hounding everybody. So I try to be as much of an external eye as possible by staying away for a couple of days, then coming in and trying to look at something with new eyes. I come in, and I usually have a decent enough relationship with the director to ask, "Why is that not working?" or "Is there something that I can do to help here?" What I really try to do in rehearsal is to just stay sensitive to what the energy is like in the room. You can sort of tell by people's body language when they're frustrated with a scene, or when you're giving an actress two different things to play and they don't jibe in any way.

When I'm writing a play I try to make sure that there's something interesting for the director and the actor on every page, and then even extend that. Why would a designer want to design this show? I see a big chunk of my job is pleasing my collaborators. I try to be sensitive to when they're frustrated in rehearsal.

The first thing I want actors to say is "I loved it." That sets a good tone, and playwrights are very paranoid. People will often point to a problem and the danger is that they tend to give you the solution, and the solution is never the right one. But if enough people refer to that point, or try something, you know that there is a problem there. The trick is to be sensitive to the fact that there's a problem and ignore their solutions. When people do offer a solution, we playwrights have to recognize that that's an enthusiastic and positive gesture, and what we have to learn to do is to say, "Hmm, well, that's a good idea." The egos are on the line.

The actors can point to discrepancies or frustrations in character. "In this scene I'm feeling that I want this guy dead, but in this scene it doesn't feel that I want him dead anymore. Why is that?" It may be just a matter of not having connected the dots, or in a worst-case scenario, maybe these dots don't connect into a coherent picture. I can run with a comment like, "I don't know what I'm playing here"; *that* I can work with.

I tend to trust the actors because they're emotional tools. In the case of a dramaturg sometimes, where it's a completely cognitive process, the head is a secondary instrument, and I tend to trust it secondarily. I tend to listen to a director more than a dramaturg, because a director has to go out there and make it work and find a way of taking that intellectual comment and distilling it into an emotional beat. The one time that a dramaturg is great is after the run-through, when you want to go off and lick your wounds; the only person that you can go off and have drinks with and piss and moan about everybody with is the dramaturg, who has this smug, "Well, yeah, I could have told you this. The play is much better just sitting on a shelf than being performed by those slime."

Audience responses are useful politically. The audience sort of wants to articulate the way they've been responding during the show. One of my first plays was a great production in a barn with squeaky seats. When the seats stopped squeaking, you knew the show was working. You can hear the energy in the audience. The stuff they'll talk about afterward in the critiques is a lot like what the actors will do. They'll point to a problem and give you a solution. You have to nod politely and think about that problem. But I understand that you get grants for doing post-play discussions and things like that, so it's part of the thing, like ball players giving out autographs. They want to see what you look like, and they want to score some points off you, and that's fair.

I don't think you can go in there and be confrontational. The best minds that I've worked with have said, "Audiences don't lie," and I believe that completely. They're not going to fake laughs and they're not going to fake attention.

In play development, impatience certainly doesn't work. Working with stupid people doesn't work. I don't mean that in a mean way, but one of the things about working with proven talent is, if they're not making it work, maybe you should change the line. Working with somebody who's impatient about fixing it can be destructive. There's certainly a time to make it performance-ready, but early on let's just see what it is that we have here.

The more you go through these processes, the better you understand how to work them. When I was in graduate school, sometimes I'd sort of wonder why we were doing something, or take some of these processes for granted, but then I realized how really golden they were. We always think that as soon as that last page comes out it's ready. It's a healthy bit of humility to talk with somebody and find out what still needs to be done.

The bugaboo that I'm working with these days is getting that fortune-cookie comment of what this play is about, that Einsteinian big theory that everything fits into. Any help that I can get, especially from a director, in helping to identify that one thing that this play is about, that's what I look for. A wise artistic director said to me once, "Well, if you don't say it the publicity department will." Sometimes I've felt that they have been reductive, but I can't think of any times when they've been completely off the mark. You look at a play like Hamlet and you can say it's about life in Denmark and it's about a political system and it's about ghosts, but what's the $E = mc^2$ to *Hamlet*? There may be a couple of ways of stating that with a masterpiece, but it's really useful to have a clear-headed, one-line description that's not reductive. I try to take that outside of theatre; I look at descriptions of TV shows, of films, or I even try to describe baseball in one sentence. The thing I'm doing with the World Cup is waiting for someone to do a one-line description of the off-sides in soccer that's clear to me.

ANN CATTANEO

Ann Cattaneo graduated from Mills College and began working in the theatre, first as an intern, and later as an assistant to Edward Hastings in the New Play Program at the American Conservatory Theatre in San Francisco. She worked as a drama critic for several underground papers in San Francisco in the late 1960s. After graduating from the Yale School of Drama with an MFA in Dramatic Literature and Criticism, she taught acting, directing, and theatre history for three years at Briarcliff College. From 1977 to 1981 she was literary manager of the Phoenix Theatre in New York, where she ran the Playworks and Commissioning Program that developed and produced such plays as Wendy Wasserstein's *Isn't It Romantic*, Mustapha Matura's *Meetings*, and Christopher Durang's *Beyond Therapy*. From 1981 through 1984, Cattaneo taught dramaturgy and dramatic literature at the University of California at San Diego, Columbia University, and the Playwrights Horizons Studio at New York University. She also worked as a freelance dramaturg with directors such as James Lapine (*A Midsummer Night's Dream* at the NYSF's Delacorte Theatre), Anne Bogart (*Danton's Death, Spring Awakening,* and *1951* at NYU and the New York Theatre Workshop), Robert Wilson (*Hamletmachine* at NYU), and Robert Falls (*Galileo* at the Goodman).

In 1985, as dramaturg of the Acting Company, Cattaneo created the touring project *Orchards: Seven Contemporary Playwrights Adapt Stories by Chekhov,* which featured short plays by Maria Irene Fornes, Spalding Gray, John Guare, David Mamet, Wendy Wasserstein, Michael Weller, and Samm-Art Williams. *Orchards* was published by Alfred A. Knopf and later by Broadway Play Publishing. She has translated a number of contemporary German plays, including Botho Strauss's *Big and Little* (published by Farrar, Straus, and Giroux). During 1986 and 1987 she was dramaturg at the Lincoln Center Theatre. She is currently serving as president of the national dramaturg's organization LMDA (Literary Managers and Dramaturgs of America).

THERE ARE a variety of ways to approach a script. When you're looking for a play that you could do in a particular space in a particular theatre, you work much along the lines of an editor in a publishing house, seeing what the writer's strengths are, and so on. That's when you're dealing with writers who might already know what they're doing, writers with some experience, where you can assume that they're conscious and capable of handling what they put down on the page. That's not at all the case when you're dealing with younger—less experienced—writers, where you may wish to point out certain things about a script so they can strengthen it in its own fashion. That's often the function of ancillary programs, like reading programs, for example, where the goal is not necessarily to come up with a product for the main stage, but simply to move a script along to its next stage of development.

If it is a play that I feel strongly about, that needs work, then I might ask the writer to come in, to meet the writer if I don't know him already, to see if we might bring him into the theatre to do a reading of the play, or to do some work on the play in the future. That would really begin the process of work on the script. It's really when you feel there's something strong that's going on in the script. When I teach this, I always ask my students to write their initial responses to a script to describe the two best things about each play, the two strongest things about the play, and then the two weakest things about the play.

One's attempt is to strengthen the strongest things—to take the cues that the author has given you, so that you don't try to get Samuel Beckett to write like Neil Simon, or vice versa— they can't, they just do the thing that they do. You don't try to codify the plays that you work on, to the way that *you* work. You must remain flexible to what the author has given you.

Once you decide to undertake a process with a writer, it's a long and ongoing process, which starts with meeting the writer, reading the other works of the writer, talking to the writers about who they read, who they're interested in, so that you can pick up some cues about what they're trying to do. You begin to get some sense when you're working for the first time with a writer of how much they're conscious of doing, how much they're in control of, how much they know what's happening. With writers of experience, the wonderful thing is that they know exactly what's going on. With fledgling writers that's not always the case.

Then you begin to make very tentative suggestions. I always phrase it, "Let me give you a reading about what I see happening here. You don't have to *do* it." The pressure that writers feel when confronted with someone who's in theatre administration is enormous, and it's very destructive. That's been a real down side of our profession, that we have injured a lot of plays by giving bad advice to playwrights who have followed that advice to get a production. One has to be very careful about that. The phrasing that I always use is, "Here's what I'm feeling about it, take it or leave it. That's a piece of information. You may want to follow it up or not."

The model for these suggestions for me has always been that a car is stranded on the side of a road in the desert. You come along, and you don't drive the car. You point out, "By the way, you've got a jack in your trunk." Or, "There's a gas station a mile down the road." Whether that person decides to go to that gas station, to walk, or to drive on a flat tire, or hitch-hike, or however, is up to them. You never suggest how to solve the problem, but you may point out that there are various resources or clues.

The goal is to clarify the playwright's intention, to understand the structure of the piece, and to strengthen it. The goal is always to do that work before rehearsals start. It may be possible to do that work by talking with the author.

At some point you may need to show authors what they have. I often say, "Oh, let's put it up on its feet and hear what we've got"—especially when it comes to cutting. When you hear it, you may realize that your first cut didn't work, but another way to do it may be better. Rather than just blindly go in you can show them a couple of things. That's a good way to think about it, too. You can say, "Here's my suggestion for a cut—let me just show it to you." Get some actors together, show it, and if they don't like it, fine. You're not forcing them to do it. This process is a talking and often a hearing process as well.

It's been my experience that different problems are revealed in rehearsal. The kind of actors' problems that may show up, for example, are "How do I get from here to here? What's my transition at this moment? What's the throughline of the character?" In gross terms, you think of that before you go into rehearsal, but the actual moment-to-moment energy, the moment-to-moment specifics that actors need to hang their work on, to create a role, may need to be clarified. That's the kind of stuff that comes up in rehearsal.

I think that the best kind of actor for this work is a generous actor, an actor with technique and experience who is not afraid to speak to an author and be generous with his comments. It's not about giving a performance at this point, it's about saying, "Here's what I'm feeling about the part, here's

what I'm understanding, is this what you need, is this what
you want, would you like to add to this?" People who are
caught up in their own egos to the point where they can't
speak are probably not going to be very helpful.

My first play at the Phoenix, when I was hired, was Wendy
Wasserstein's *Uncommon Women and Others*. She was right out
of school, was very young as an author. She had a marvelous
cast, many of whom were actresses she didn't know. One of
them, Swoozie Kurtz, was sort of a star. I remember watching
Swoozie working with Wendy. Swoozie was such an experienced actress, so brilliant, and she would gently say, "I love
this moment. I wonder what it would be like if I tried it in a
reverse order? 'You know what I mean? Let's go out the door'
instead of 'Let's go out the door. You know what I mean?' If
you don't like it, I'll put it back." She did it in a very gentle
fashion, and she had such stage experience that she could
make a line pay off. Wendy learned a lot from that. Swoozie
did it in a very wonderful way. Wendy was the author and
Swoozie would never dream of telling her how to do this;
she'd say, "Let me show you this," the way she'd say to a
director, "Let me try it this way, see what you think." She did
it with the author as well. That's a really good example of the
kind of thing I'm talking about.

Again, you have to be careful because a lot of actors may
just wish to increase the size of their parts, so it really depends
on a group of collaborators who are friends and who you can
trust. The more dialogue between actors and playwrights the
better. I always encourage the actors: "What do you think,
tell me what you feel about doing that," and so on.

Usually you just turn them loose in a reading. It's very
instructive when you send actors a script for a reading and
ask them to come in and read it cold. It's instructive to see
how they prepare. What they come in with the first time will
tell the writer what clues the writer has planted in the work.
If an actor comes in and does something totally wrong, there's

usually a reason for it. They've picked up a false clue. Thus, talking to them before the reading gets in the way of their spontaneous responses.

I think you have to use an audience very carefully, for two reasons. One is the general tendency in our culture to see art, theatre, as being something that anybody can do. "I'll just come in as an audience member and give you my opinion." You'd never go into an operating room and say to a brain surgeon, "Put that suture there," but you wouldn't think twice about going into a theatre and saying, "Cut that out." That's a tendency that must be discouraged in all ways.

I've always used audience discussions in the following way. In early previews of a new play, I will do a discussion often without the author, although the author may be sitting in the audience. You welcome the audience in, tell them you're glad they're there, say they're part of a process. I'll ask the audience factual questions. I don't ever like to ask the audience what they thought—"Did you like it or not?" But I like to say, "Was there anything that confused you in watching this piece to-night? Something you didn't understand? Did you understand the thing about the letter?"

Often you find plot points that are unclear. That's when the audience is at their best. Often the audience is your best ally, when you've been saying to the author all the way through, "You know, no one gets the fact that—" and then the audience comes in and says, "Well, what happened there?" Lots of times authors bring a lot of information in their head to a play that may not be on a page, thinking that everybody will know that their Aunt So-and-So was once involved in this, and it's not at all apparent when you come to it fresh.

Sometimes there may be production things. We did a production where there was a very abstract set, and there was a park bench, and nobody got the fact that it was in this park, that confused them. Those kind of pieces of information are very helpful. The worst kind of audience discussion is when you put a playwright up and the audience says, "I didn't like it." Well, what's the author going to say? "I'm sorry"? You try to avoid making it personal in that way.

There are many ways and models to write a play. The way that we know today—which is primarily psychologically based and starts in Ibsen and ends in television in a way—is the way that we all assume plays are when we don't think carefully about it. You need to ask yourself afresh each time, what kind of a writer is this? Is this a writer who's trying to write an Ibsen play, or is this a writer who's trying to write a Dario Fo play, or a Euripides play, or a Brecht, or a Molière, or a commedia dell'arte play? What are the models of this? One of the best qualifications to work on a play is a knowledge of theatre history, a knowledge of how a Greek play worked. Not just the structure of the play, but how it fit into society, how it used the space, its function. Maybe going to the plays then was like going to a psychiatrist today, or going to church, so you went in with different expectations. You must think and question all those basic assumptions.

I had an experience once with Steve Tesich. He sent me a play, and I hate to admit this, but I just wasn't thinking. It was a play in process, a new work. There was a central character I was really held at a distance from. When I read it I was held back. I never should have said this, but I said to him, "Well, we need a way into this character. She needs to be more sympathetic." He said, "Would you say that to Brecht about Mother Courage?" Of course I would never say that to Brecht. I would be making a total travesty of not only that play, but that approach to the theatre. I was mortified. He was of course absolutely right.

So you must be careful to see what the models are, what's trying to be done. Sometimes you want to close the fourth wall, sometimes you want to open it up. Other times you want to make something completely self-conscious. There are so many different ways to go. The best times are when you perceive that an author is going for something and you know a script that does it even better in history. You can say, "Why don't you pick up this Peter Handke, or this play by Plautus." It's exciting to see how other playwrights have solved similar problems.

The major piece of advice I would give to a director is that you must treat every script as if it were the original manuscript of *Waiting for Godot*—with that kind of respect and that kind of caution. You are in your career in the hopes that that will come to you some day—a script that is brilliant and that you don't understand yet and that you can learn and grow as an artist to understand and realize. If you ever stop thinking like that, you are going to start butchering your script.

The worst danger is thinking that you know the answer to something, and not allowing the work to take you someplace that you've never been.

OSKAR EUSTIS

Oskar Eustis is Artistic Director of Trinity Repertory Company of Providence, Rhode Island. As director of play development for the Mark Taper Forum, he directed *Angels in America* and *Julius Caesar* on the mainstage and *Millennium Approaches* at Taper Too. He also directed the world premieres of David Henry Hwang's *Bondage* and Susan-Lori Park's *Devotees in the Garden of Love* for Actors Theatre of Louisville, and Philip Kan Gotanda's *Day Standing on Its Head* at Manhattan Theatre Club. He spent the 1980s first as dramaturg and later artistic director of the Eureka Theatre in San Francisco, where he directed world premieres of works by Philip Gotanda, Ellen McLaughlin, Tony Kushner, and Emily Mann, among others. He has directed at Berkeley Rep, San Jose Rep, Trinity Rep, and numerous other regional theatres in America and Europe, where he spent two years as founder of the "Labor," the laboratory second stage of the Schauspielhaus Zurich in Switzerland. He chairs the playwrights panel of the NEA and has been a regular participant at the Sundance

Festival in Utah and Midwest Playlabs in Minnesota. He served on the faculty of UCLA's School of Theatre, Film, and Television. In 1992, he was awarded the "Most Valuable Straight Guy" award by Tim Miller.

WORKING ON *Execution of Justice* by Emily Mann was the most complete developmental project imaginable because we started with nothing, we started from an idea, and Emily and I sort of took every step together. We ended up figuring we had been in nine cities working on it. We did interviews, we researched raw material, we spent our Christmas vacations together going over [the Dan White] trial transcripts. We really put together not just the script itself but what for me is the most important aspect of working on any play—whether you're the playwright or not the playwright—figuring out what we thought about the whole thing, what it was all about.

I think that's what it's about: trying to get a sense of the basic event you're writing about, not in a theatrical sense but in a real sense, and, on the other hand, holding someone's hand, going down in the trenches with someone who's engaged in one of the most lonely and difficult endeavors— writing a play. Playwriting is the most intensely private part of this very social art. As such, it really is the hardest thing I can imagine doing in the arts. The respect I have for playwrights is enormous.

An important aspect of the work is helping to provide a bridge for playwrights between the privacy of the act and the publicness of what will eventually be a production. You give solace, understanding, dialogue—a safe person to have a dialogue with can be tremendously important to a lot of playwrights, somebody who is absolutely on their side and with whom they can feel some sense of real trust.

During the developmental process the director constantly redefines his role based on what is helpful—and he's not the one deciding that. Ultimately it's the writer who decides that. If you're not doing the writer any good, you're not doing your job. Every writer needs different things and every writer needs different things at different times. You have to be fundamentally responsive to that, and sympathetic to that, and understanding of that. It's both an attitude and a talent that you develop over the years.

What I'm looking for in a new script is whether the play excites me to think, touches me, seems to offer something. It's a feeling more than anything else. I've learned to trust that.

I know a lot of people who have developed fairly thick concepts of play development and what plays should have. They'll look for the underlying spine, the clarity of the central action, the movement and objectives of the characters, the clarity of the climax, and yada yada yada yada yada. Well, fine. I think those are interesting tools to have in my bag. I also know there are plays that have all of those things and are completely uninteresting. And I know there are plays that have none of those things obviously and yet totally speak to me. So, what I'm looking for is a unique voice, a voice that seems to be speaking some truth; it's not an imitation of other plays, or an imitation of a textbook, or an idea of what they would like to be true, but it is somehow speaking from their true perception of reality. That I understand. At that point I say, "I don't give a shit if the throughline is completely clear or if the central action is there, there's something to work with and we can make something happen in a dialogue."

My next step is to figure out if there's any way to really work on it. I firmly believe that you don't ask writers to just start working on a script with you because you're so cute. You've got to be able to offer them something. The fundamental thing that a director has to offer playwrights is opportunity—opportunity for a production. You can offer playwrights opportunities for development as well, but I try to be very clear about that transaction.

Before we go through the script, we usually just start talking about the show, and the question I always ask is, "When did you start writing the show and why did you start writing it?" Not "justify this," but just "tell me what you were thinking about." I always say, "What were you reading when you wrote this play? Whether it had anything to do with the play or not, what were you reading?" And then I read it. You'll usually find that that's the key to something. With certain writers it's "What movies have you seen, or what music were you listening to?" But again, you get into the world, you start to understand the beats and rhythm of it. That's really important. And usually if you can get somebody to really start talking about that, you open up Pandora's box; that's when you start getting into the real heart of the play.

Lee Breuer said something to me when I was a kid that has always impressed me: "You make theatre about subjects that give you the energy to keep making theatre." It's certainly true of writing a play. If you can tap into writers' sources of energy, what it is that fascinates them or compels them so much that they're willing to engage in the insane process of sitting there trying to write a play, you're way ahead of the game.

Then, we go through the play and, if I have my druthers, sit and read it together. We'll read a page and talk about it a little bit, I'll ask questions, we'll read another page, I'll ask some more questions. And when I don't understand something or think something isn't working, I'll just ask questions and try to understand as completely as possible what the playwright's strategy is. "Why is that person saying this here?" I always assume there's some reason I don't understand it. It makes me so angry when directors assume that the playwright hasn't thought of it. Well, damn it, if a playwright's spent the one thousand hours, or whatever it is, he or she's probably thought about it, there's probably a reason the playwright's doing it. It may be wrong, it may not work, the playwright may have conflicting reasons, may not even like what it is. You may ask, "What's going on here?" and the playwright will say, "Oh, I hate that part, it doesn't work, does it?" But very often, no matter how smart you are, the playwright has an intention that you have not completely understood—everything from the overall intention of the play to the individual beats. And again, I try to understand that as thoroughly as possible.

Of course, then there's the dilemma of ownership. Generally, the playwright owns the play and the director doesn't, and you've got to have that absolutely clear in your mind when you're working. If you don't, if you try to get your fingerprints all over somebody else's work, it's going to lead to nothing but tension, heartbreak, broken relationships, and disappointment—and people bitterly talking about how their careers never did what they expected them to do. It's a relationship of love in that way.

Amlin [Gray] says, "You have to be careful about getting the stink of your ideas on the playwright's work." The best bet is always to empower the playwright. This is why I like the structure at Sundance so much—it's the idea that the playwright's in charge, the playwright gets to say what we're going to do in rehearsal today. It's a wonderful tool. That's what you're depending on as a director, because any idea that the playwright doesn't completely embrace and own is not going to be of any use in rewriting the play.

I think there are some directors—they may be purer directors than I am—who I think are wonderful showmen but who are useless in play development precisely because what they are trying to do is make the show work. That's not how I work and that's not how most good play development works. What you've got to hold to is the playwright's vision of how the play is going to work. You try to make it work that way. If it does, great! If it doesn't, you've found out something. In production, it's different. You can say, "I don't think the way the playwright imagined this is going to be as effective as the way I can reimagine it." Occasionally that's true.

Every playwright's different, and you've got to learn how to talk to them. With most playwrights, there's not a percentage in arguing with them. When you're in an argument, you're in trouble. It's just like a director's relationship to actors: you never win an argument with an actor. If the actor doesn't win the argument, everybody loses. The actors need to feel that they are powerful and can do something; same with the playwright.

With other playwrights you don't even need to worry about that for a second. They consider that they have certain objective intentions, and by God if the play isn't working that way they want to know about it and they want to talk about what you think about it, and they'll goddamn-well rewrite it until it says that.

For all my talk about listening and giving over and being humble, there obviously is expertise that is associated with this process. I know I would be a far worse developmental director if I didn't really know the Aristotelian unities, if I didn't really know Brecht's epic structure, or if I didn't really have a lot of theoretical knowledge about how other plays have worked. I have those things as tools because there are certain basic principles of playwriting that may not be universally true but *are* universally true in our perception. And if we're going to contradict that, we're going to immediately set up a tension. An example of this is central action: if you do a play without a central action, there are going to be certain consequences that you've got to be prepared to deal with. If you don't have a protagonist, you're going to have a lot of work. If the climax of the play does not involve an action on the part of the protagonist but involves the protagonist as essentially a passive onlooker, that's going to cause a lot of complications.

Your audience is educated, consciously or unconsciously, in those things too. That's what we think of as a play; it's a social contract, it's not something that's a private, individual thing. That's what genre is: it's a contract between us and the audience and if we're going to change the terms of that we have to take responsibility for it and make sure we follow through on the consequences.

That's exactly what the playwright wants too. I've never met a playwright who didn't care whether his or her work communicated to an audience. A playwright cares about it passionately—more than you do. It's not something you have to give to the playwright or you have to fight the playwright about. Once you're into an honest dialogue, the playwright trusts you and will keep asking how it will work. They listen, and they care about that, and they'll try to find an answer.

The ideal play development situation is one where you have actors available whenever you want them and not available when you want them to go away. That doesn't happen very often.

The structures that work best are ones that involve the actors at some point in the workshop process, either after the first draft is done or at the beginning of the process before the play is written when you are collectively developing and improvising. That's worked very well for Caryl Churchill and Joint Stock Company: you have six weeks together to improvise and whatever else, you have three months off for the writer to write, and then you have the extended rehearsal period. That's idyllic. Most of us can't afford that.

The first time you do a reading with actors it's always the same: read it for content. What's most helpful is if actors are thinking their way through the text. They're not trying to perform, they're just trying to get what it's about.

The second thing you try to encourage is for everybody to ask questions: "Why does this guy say this? Is there a reason he uses this word? This has just been said to him, why isn't he responding? Why is he talking to his mom rather than just jumping? Why am I exiting here?" These shouldn't be rhetorical questions, but real questions with answers. Now that answer might be, "I don't know, I was just trying to get you off stage." And then you can say, "Well, I think we'd better look at it; that's not a very good reason."

I try to facilitate as much actor contact with the playwright as possible on the principle that it empowers the playwright. You should not be protecting the playwright from people's feedback any more than you should be protecting the actors from hearing what the playwright thinks.

Then we do a lot of really breaking down scenes; sometimes that means putting a scene on its feet and sometimes it doesn't. It means just trying to understand a scene as fully as possible, using actors to understand every intention. That's the point where I start to do some directing—checking with the playwright: "Does this feel right?" "Yeah, yeah, yeah," Or "No, I don't see it that way." And as soon as they're not seeing it that way you say, "Why? What do you see differently?" Sometimes they'll say something you never thought of and you'll say, "Oh, I get it now. Do it this way." Sometimes they'll say something and you'll say, "Well, yeah, I see that you want that to happen but it really can't because of the scene you wrote before." Or, "I can't, because I can't see where the text is there to do that." And then you have a dialogue going about it.

Some of the most valuable work I've done in play development incorporated discussions with actors not on the level of throughlines and objectives but on the level of "What's this play about?" Almost always, in an extended play development process, we'll have one long session where we just sit and talk about what we think the play's about, why we like it, what it reminds us of. Everybody gets more invested, and it clarifies the thing you always have to go back to, which is, what's the basic theme of this work? You're clarifying it and solidifying it, giving the writer a social context. You're giving the writer the privacy aspects of not being criticized, of not being judged, of not having production pressure, with the social aspect of having a bunch of different minds talking about the things they care about.

The function of the actors and the director is to use any way possible to give the playwright the clearest possible vision of the work—warts and all. Sometimes putting it on its feet is useful, though I usually don't think it is. I find that staging it script in hand is a real hybrid thing that forces actors to start faking a lot of stuff. The most helpful thing actors can do is to try to turn in the most honest performance of the material they can.

If you have an audience, listen to what they have to say. Always give the playwrights the choice of not being there. They occasionally take it, and sometimes I think it's the best thing in the world if they do, because at a minimally rehearsed reading you never know what your audience is going to get. If the playwright's not there, or if the audience doesn't know the playwright is there, they'll just say what they think of the experience. That's much more valuable to you than their saying, "I think the president should die in act 2." But if everybody is saying, "You know, the first scene in the second act didn't work," I'll listen to that. Audiences aren't stupid.

You have to assume an intelligent audience; you have to assume an audience that also cares about things like the integrity of the work. When audiences don't like stuff, it's an indication of something. I'm not saying when it's not popular—you can do shows that certain people will hate and certain people will love, but if everybody in the audience is squirming in act 2, scene 2, then something's not working.

What I try to do in readings is make the rules absolutely clear to the audience, not only what we say but also how the reading is set up: it's clear that it's a reading, that the actors have made some choices, that the stage manager's reading stage directions. This gives the audience the best chance of focusing on what you're focusing on: the central issues of the text.

You also keep in continual contact with the playwright. Hopefully, by the time we actually get a production scheduled, I've enough of a relationship going with the playwright that we're talking all the time about the play and what to do with it and how to work with it and if he or she's going to write it more. By that point, you've got to have clarity about the division of labor and responsibility: every word spoken on stage—or not spoken on stage—is ultimately the playwright's choice, every directorial and design choice is ultimately the director's choice. Without that clarity I think relationships can get really screwy. You just have to hope you agree, because ultimately the play is only going to be as good as your relationship is.

ROBERT HEDLEY

Robert Hedley has worked with playwrights since graduate school in the 1960s. At Villanova he met and worked with David Rabe and Leslie Lee, among others. He was a co-founder of the Philadelphia Company, which was dedicated to developing and producing new work, and co-founder of West Coast Playwrights, a developmental workshop. For nine years he was director of the Iowa Playwrights Workshop and artistic director of its Playwrights Festival. He has been on panels, advised arts organizations, adjudicated, and otherwise promoted new play development. Hedley directed new work at a variety of theatres, including the New York Shakespeare Festival, La Mama, Theatre 46 of New York, Marin Theatre Company, and the Philadelphia Company. Writers he worked with have won most of the major awards and grants. Recently he created a new program for advanced playwrights at Temple University in Philadelphia.

I'VE APPROACHED play development from two points of view: as a director/artistic director working with writers on projects that I had some direct part in producing and as a mentor/teacher during the years I headed the Iowa Playwrights workshop. Although I continue to direct new plays, my preference in "development" is working with writers without also thinking about productions I might do. It's cleaner and, I think, more likely to help a play end up closer to the playwright's vision.

When I think about "play development" I mean the earliest stages of a play's life; the writer has done a draft or two but the play doesn't do what the writer wants it to do, when the writer is groping for the play's form.

In development what you're trying to do is encourage what is unique about a writer. You're trying not to be directive, but you're saying, "All right, here's part of your play that seems really interesting and working and all that kind of thing, where did it come from, what were you dealing with?" What are procedures to get the writer writing more?

So the first task is to find out what that person thinks she or he is writing, what they have on the page, what's in their mind, what it came from, where it all started. When you're involved in a play, what you're trying to do is get back to the real sources, the creative time, when the writing wasn't hard, when it was easy, when it had an idea that really seemed important to investigate.

So the first stage is sitting down and finding out what the playwright wants to write, what their play is. It's real simple. A lot of people don't pay any attention to the process of generating the play. They don't have the notion that the playwright's idea is probably better than their own idea.

It's very simple to be a play doctor, to say, "Change this," and so on. That kind of advice, which is much of what you get in the theatre, almost guarantees plays that are adequate in theme and structure but that are mediocre in the long haul, because they're not individual, they're not idiosyncratic, they're "community written."

Play development is a one-on-one proposition, not a bunch of different people offering different advice; it's sort of quiet and humble rather than everyone demonstrating how bright they are.

Most new plays are changed in rehearsal but the "development" time that is most crucial occurs before rehearsals ever begin. It's the time when huge changes can be made, the most exciting time. "Development" in the best sense is making the writer's ideas blossom. Not being overly concerned with shape but trying to assist in getting the best stuff out of the writer's head and onto the page.

Some years ago, I spent a good deal of time traveling around looking at new play productions. As part of the process I always included a private talk with the playwright. What goes on in the name of development, especially if the playwright is powerless, as she or he usually is, can be dreadful. I remember commenting to one writer that a particular scene didn't seem to fit the style of the rest. "Of course not," he said, "I didn't write it."

Some people, directors in particular, often don't understand that the playwright is the play, that the vision of the play is not its "idea" or something else that can be deconstructed or otherwise reconstituted . . . something beyond the cut and paste arrogance of script adapters. Usually a writer is chasing something as transitory as style or the special nuances of a moment in someone's history. The "material" will be banal without that particular viewpoint on it. The musicality, say, may be more important than the idea. That viewpoint translated into good craft will give the material power and resonance that are completely surprising and individual.

My objection to much "development" is that it resembles real estate development. Something raw is made efficient. Efficiency usually means conforming to established play forms or chopping off what is perplexing or ambiguous. The shaping that goes on is an attempt, in the worst instances, to make something unruly behave. Too often the process is an exercise in making things "work."

It is true that when I am going to direct a play that I am working with the writer on, I find myself imagining how the bits and pieces will "work" and what can be done to make them "work" better. It is a natural tendency, I think, to give in to one's expertise and unconsciously short-circuit the writing process. It is also true that sometimes these directorial ideas can be very helpful. It's a matter of knowing when an idea is supportive and when the director is turning the writer into a typist. Later, when the piece has found its shape and the writer is "written out," these directorial ideas may be more valuable and can be springboards to helpful rewrites.

I think that when I am working well with a writer I am the alter ego for the writer, someone who will not pass judgment on it but who will be resistant to easy solutions. I know that I have been poorest when I have become more invested in certain ideas and characters than the writer. You may win arguments about a lot of things, a scene, a line, a character, but in my experience, you often lose the play or at least the opportunity to see a terrific play written.

I like to hear plays read first of all by the playwrights, other playwrights, amateurs, and then eventually getting up to professional actors. Initially at least you get a reading and certain acting that is sort of flat. You hear it, so you get that aural treatment, but it isn't overpowered by certain actors.

The acting has to be quick. There can't be any time for deep acting. In the initial reading you need to really go for it and be daring. Do as much as you can in a reading, even if it is at times a little hammy. That's all right, because the worst thing that can happen at a first reading is for the actors to take it extraordinarily seriously and be heavily acting it, pausing, deep emotions. You're not looking for that in a first reading.

In a reading, you're looking for how lively did it feel, how is this voice joining in with this voice, this scene colliding with that scene, how stimulating was it? Did I walk into that reading feeling lively and walk out feeling dull, even if the intellectual content of it seems to be quite stimulating? What you're doing in that sort of reading is measuring how the room breathes as people listen to this. You know, people won't articulate, they don't understand, what was interesting about a piece; they'll point out the obvious, that this climactic action, this stabbing was interesting. But if you listen to the room, you know when they're listening.

The head of the critic's institute at the O'Neill once said

that he didn't think it was possible for anyone to separate acting from text. In other words, if we do a reading here and now and somebody reads particularly well, really zeroes in and can be an interesting counterpoint to the dialogue, virtually everybody who makes comments will say things like, "That's an interesting character, I don't think you should eliminate that character." No matter how trivial the role in the text is, most people will define the play in terms of how well that actor worked, and that goes for experienced people, too. If you get the wrong actor in the leading role, they're bound to mention that the leading role just isn't interesting enough, that you should rewrite the role so the leading character does more.

You're looking for a balanced approach to the acting. You're reading, doing a lot of guessing, then you need an actor who has tremendous concentration, a person who really will attempt to make the lines work, not wait for the inspiration to hit, but rather work the text, and be real, and commit themselves, and many actors are not like that.

At Iowa, the writer brings in a script, and with me or the playwright-in-residence, we do talks until we've gone about as far as we can go one-to-one. Then we have at least an informal and probably a formal reading. At the formal reading there's an audience—other people who are not necessarily connected to it—the actors, other directors, other playwrights, the author, everybody talks about it in public. Then we go back with the writers and talk about it in private, which may or may not be the same result. In the public reading what we say to the people is, all we want to know is what was your response: Were you bored? Did you want it to be more specific? You liked this character, didn't like this character. All these things are raw input and are useful.

Then we did a debriefing with the playwright with the two of us in which we say things like, "Well, what did you learn? What's going to be your rewriting emphasis?" The debriefing was to try to remove the clutter and get to the important comments, to find the consensus.

Then after that there was another rewrite. Often, after two more rewrites, it will go into a workshop. A workshop production meant that they cast it, that there's a director, a designer, a couple of hundred dollars budget. More rewriting went on during the workshop. After that the play might be chosen for the playwrights festival or for a main stage production. At its best the process allowed for a number of different opportunities to work on rewrites, to make the play work as well as it could.

Directing new work has its own hazards. At a certain point you go into a period when the play is awful. If you go into that middle period in Shakespeare, you say to yourself, "It's my problem, it's the actor's problem, if we work hard we can get it." With a new play, you get to that stage and you say, "The play's not right." So your solution is massive rewrites; you wouldn't do that if it were Shakespeare.

Sometimes you just can't make things work. That happens in most plays and maybe half of the time you're right. Half of the time it will work if you work at it hard enough. I usually follow the procedure of just being honest with the playwright and saying "Look, I can't make that thing work. What is the idea of it? What am I missing? Can you tell me where it came from?" I try to examine it as a problem in myself.

Play "development" obviously can be a helpful process. Very fine plays have survived it, and nowadays few plays get up without some form of it. There are also some terrific people working in development . . . whose humility allows them to put the writer first.

MORGAN JENNESS

Morgan Jenness has spent almost fifteen years working in play development and production dramaturgy in the American theatre. She started at the New York Shakespeare Festival/Public Theatre, where she worked from 1979 to 1988 with Joseph Papp and Gail Merrifield in capacities ranging from play reader, literary manager, assistant director, and production dramaturg, to associate director of play development and artistic consultant. From 1989 to 1990, she was associate artistic director of the New York Theatre Workshop and co-head of the New Directors Project.

Jenness moved to Los Angeles to serve as an associate director at the now-defunct Los Angeles Theatre Center in 1990–91, where she was in charge of literary development, booking performances in Theatre 4, and overseeing six multicultural development and training labs, as well as serving as production dramaturg and as a line producer of the annual spring Festival of New Work. In 1992, after spending two years freelancing, she returned to the Joseph Papp Public Theatre to work with George C. Wolfe as director of play development.

Jenness has spent ten years working with the Young Playwrights Festival as a screening committee member, dramaturg/advisor, and workshop leader. She has been a site visitor for the National Endowment for the Arts, for theater organizations, and solo performance artists, as well as serving as a reader for the playwriting grants. Jenness also works as a panel member and advisor to the Drama League Directors Program. She has worked as a dramaturg and developmental director at various theatres and programs across the country and has been a visiting professor/guest artist at the University of Iowa, New York University, and Brown University.

THE MAIN THING, and a very important thing, which amazingly is not done a lot, is to find out how the playwright sees the play. I've gone into situations where they've had readings and more readings and no one has ever sat down and talked to them about how they see the play. You can really get into trouble if you make assumptions. Everyone thinks they see the same things. It's not necessarily true. The most important thing is to make sure you're looking at the same animal.

A lot of times writers can't really talk about what they meant when they wrote something. So you ask questions—what the strongest part is for them, what was the trigger for the play? You talk about some of your notions and see whether they look at you like you're nuts or whether it triggers things in them. You make sure that the basic essence or the heartbeat of the work is mutually understood. Whether or not they can put it into words—"my play is about this"—doesn't matter, as long as we're both looking at the same thing and coming from the same place. Then dealing with their intent, with what they wanted, I say, "Well, if you wanted *this*, then here is where it doesn't work for me, here's where I get lost, here is where I feel something is missing." We talk a lot about why that is, whether they feel similarly. This opens up areas of investigation.

Sometimes it's a question that you can't answer until you get into rehearsal with actors, because if the intent is clear, maybe it *is* there, and you need to find it working with the actors. Sometimes it's a question that can be addressed before rehearsal with rewrites, in which case it's good to try to do it then, because it does save some time. It's always good to go in with the strongest script possible, before rehearsal. Then you can just dig deeper.

There's a lot of talking. Sometimes these conversations confirm notions that have been sitting in their head and they'll just go ahead and do it. Sometimes they want to hear it. A lot of times I'll say, "You don't have to do anything, but think about these things for the first read-through." I like to have a lot of questions in the air by the first read-through.

A lot depends on the time framework and on the goals of the process. If you're putting a show up, it's going to be in front of critics and audience in two months, it's a different approach than if you have a first draft and no one's quite sure exactly in which direction it could conceivably go.

I've never been out there, but I understand that Sundance [Institute] was a very good place for that, because it's a very closed environment, there are no performance goals, no public presentation, no outside audience, so it really is an incubator time where someone can take something and experiment with the actors there and ask questions and really investigate a piece internally. That's a very luxurious process. For a work in the beginning, it's fabulous. You can go with all that input and either use it or not. The lack of pressure is really good. You don't make quick choices for presentation. I like to do that kind of work, that's just about investigating, experimental investigating language, like theatrical language, that's wonderful. These situations need to exist.

Then there are processes like the O'Neill and Midwest Play Labs, where the public presentation is really a part of it. The script is in enough of a solid understanding of what it is that it can be challenged by the pressure of a public performance.

Generally you're headed towards having it in front of an audience. So at some point the pressure of a public presentation is good, because you start including the thought of them into the equation. It's not geared totally toward the audience, it's not all about questions of clarity, whether things are going to come across—it's still about investigation, but there's a balance. It's about investigation, but you have a little pressure against indulgence, against investigation for just investigation's sake. The issue of *communication* becomes stronger.

For a developmental process, intelligent actors are always the best. It's tricky, because you want actors who will ask a *lot* of questions, but you want actors who will ask the *right* questions of the writer. It's a problem if they get off on their own theory of the play—everyone's always trying to write their own play, and actors are as prone to this as anyone else, but the kind of questions that the actor asks about the character from the *inside* are just incredibly valuable. Like, "I don't know how I get from A to B. I'm here and I've just said this. What happens here?" These questions do not necessarily have to be *answered* by the playwright. But the fact that the question is being asked, opens up, "Well, is it being addressed?" A lot of times you decide yes, it is being addressed, and that it's a directorial approach that can make it jump into focus.

For two or three rehearsals, where it's just a quick thing, you try to get the main intents of each character, what each character wants, their ultimate intent, and real broad strokes of their relationships to other characters—what they feel about each other, and what they're going toward. You just want to have the play move from beginning to end. You lose out on a lot of the subtlety and the colorations in the read-through, but you get the primary colors. You give them primary colors basically.

It's hard, because there are certain types of questions that kind of reading will answer, and there are certain it won't. If it's a very straightforward psychological play, sometimes it will answer questions about where there are gaps, where there are things we don't know, where the plot falls out, where a relationship isn't totally explored, where we don't have enough information or signals that prepare us for what happens later, where we get lost in the broad map of the play, where we just left out this whole city. It can be good for that.

However, the more the play is fragmented, nontraditional, nonlinear, and deals with juxtapositions, the less helpful that is going to be. The more you need phrasing—musical phrasing of text, or movement—the harder it's going to be. One of the problems in the theatre right now is that there are so many readings that are happening—because there are fewer productions—plays are almost being written for readings. That's a real danger, because the type of work that could be the most interesting you really can't see until you have actors and you're on your feet. That's the biggest frustration.

A longer rehearsal process always makes it better, because you have more time to sit at the beginning, to dig. Some people like to sketch the outline of the whole play with the actors. Some like to work scene by scene. It depends on the actors you have and it depends on the director's taste. I've worked with playwrights who wanted to see a quick sketch of the play up on its feet right away. If you don't like to work that way, if you like to examine each little piece as you get it, you have a problem sometimes.

In a developmental situation you have to give over to what the playwright needs and put the way you work outside. There are negotiations that can go on. In rehearsal you sort of make a deal. You agree what you are going to go after. The playwright will try not to judge how you're getting it. Sometimes you'll give an actor a direction about a character that won't seem to be the main aspect about that character. But you don't need to give them the main thing, because maybe they have that already. What they need to work on is another aspect of the character that's not the motivating aspect but that needs to be in there to make it work. A lot of times writers will say, "But that's not the character." You just make a deal with the playwright that unless they think you're on the wrong track in what you're going after, they'll try to hold back and not panic. When I feel that I have something sketched out that is a sense of what I want, I'll check and make sure—"Is this what you want?"

I think I'm pretty smart and I get a lot of things, but sometimes—you appreciate the play a lot more while you're working on it—sometimes something will come up that hasn't occurred to either one of you. A play's very much a live thing and you're all responsible to it. It even takes precedence over the writers themselves. You're all responsible to this living entity. The more it becomes alive, the more it is like a child, it develops its own personality, its own needs. They become very apparent. When you fight against them, it becomes very apparent.

The needs are dictated so strongly that it's almost like listening to the voice of the work itself. It says, "I need something different from the actor here, I need something different from the writer here. I need something different from you." You just sensitize yourself to listen to it. You have your ideas of it, but your ideas have to serve it, and that's hard. If you're someone brilliant, if you're Peter Sellars, you have ideas and you take something and it becomes malleable to those ideas. I love Peter's work, but that's not the type of work you're doing in a developmental situation.

The audience is very much a part of the equation, because you watch them. The audience a lot of times is the ultimate dramaturg. It's not that they have to get everything, that everything has to be spelled out, but they do have to be interested—as Lloyd [Richards] says, you listen to the fannies. It's a very important aspect. When you get into work with young playwrights, when you get into a preview situation, lots of times I really shut up, and say, "Just listen and watch. Try to get your skin sensitized to what's going on in the house." It's the play *and* the audience. Something different happens. It's not just the play anymore.

Sometimes you have a wonderful experience, but it's only been for the people involved in the process. Everyone's happy and they have wonderful ideas and we all feel good about ourselves, but it goes up in front of an audience and the audience kind of sits there. It could be the most potentially wonderful thing, but if everyone sits out there in the audience and it doesn't reach them, that's not theatre.

But that does *not* mean our job is to compromise the work! I've seen audiences watch things that are very difficult, very experimental, that they don't totally understand, but they're *with* it. You can have the audience speak a whole different language by the end of the play, be in a whole different country than they've ever been to. But if you're going to do that, you have to make sure that you give them the vocabulary. Meredith Monk did this piece—not really a play—called *Specimen Days*. At the beginning someone came out and tied a blue ribbon around one of the actors and said, "This is a black child," they put a red beret on another actor and said, "This is a white woman." It was beautifully done. The piece was very refracted and difficult but the audience was with it because they had been given enough pieces to make their way through it.

What happens in a lot of [post-show] discussions is that the audience starts quibbling with the intent, "Why didn't they get back together again?" They start writing their own play, and that's where it gets totally useless. Sometimes you'll get incredible, insightful response from the audience and sometimes it will just be gobbledygook. The most important thing for a playwright is to always have selective hearing. If it doesn't ring true, don't buy it just because it sounds good. Young playwrights are amazing. Sometimes they have a very clear sense of what they want it to say. The danger is that they're surrounded by a lot of people who know how to fix things, and we just want to go in and *fix* things. That doesn't help.

The biggest pitfall is falling in love with your own notions. They could be brilliant and wonderful and absolutely right in a production. The problem is that if you fall in love with them and if the playwright doesn't understand it, or if it's too soon for them, or if you're just plain wrong, it alienates you from the playwright.

The most important thing is that the playwright feels that you're on his side, on the play's side. Actually, you don't even have to be on the playwright's side, but you do have to be on the play's side; in a way you're in a mutual conspiracy to create this work.

Another big pitfall is not listening to your own questions. Sometimes you'll just have a fleeting thought about something and you dismiss it. Ask stupid questions, ask inane questions, ask questions that seem to be absolutely obvious. Sometimes they're not. I've been in a situation where everyone involved with it assumed that a play was taking a certain thrust and it wasn't at all. As soon as we made the adjustment, we realized that this play that we thought was this epic intense profound thing was really much more of a black whimsical comedy. Therefore the choices to be made with it took a whole different track.

Assumptions should always be taken with a grain of salt. Constant checking. Just questions, questions, every question you can think of. Ask "What if?" a lot. You have to love what you're doing.

ROMULUS LINNEY

Romulus Linney is the author of three novels, thirteen long and twenty-two short plays, which have been seen over the past twenty-five years in resident theatres across the United States, as well as in New York, Los Angeles, London, and Vienna. They include *The Sorrows of Frederick*, *Holy Ghosts*, *Childe Byron*, *April Snow*, and *Three Poets*. Six of his one-act plays have appeared in *Best Short Plays* series. *Time* magazine picked *Laughing Stock* as one of the ten best plays of 1984. His adaptation and direction of his 1962 novel, *Heathen Valley*, won the National Critics Award and appears in *Best Plays of the Year 1987–88* and his play *"Z"* won the same award for the season of 1989–90 in its Humana Festival production at the Actors Theatre in Louisville and appears in *Best Plays of the Year 1989–90*.

Linney received two fellowships from the National Endowment for the Arts, as well as Guggenheim, Rockefeller, and National Foundation for the Arts grants, an OBIE Award, three Hollywood Drama-Logue Awards, the Mishima Prize for Fiction, and in 1984, the Award in Literature from the American Academy and Institute of Arts and Letters. He has directed his plays for the Milwaukee Repertory, the Alley Theatre, the Philadelphia Festival for New Plays, the Whole Theatre Company, the San Francisco Bay Area Festival, the Actors Studio, the Theatre for the New City, and the Signature Company. Works for film and television include *The Thirty-fourth Star* for CBS, *Feeling Good* for PBS, and a film version of his play *Holy Ghosts*. Linney is also a member of the Ensemble Studio Theatre, the Fellowship of Southern Writers, and a director of the Corporation of Yaddo. A graduate of Oberlin College and the Yale School of Drama, he is a Professor of the Arts at Columbia University and Adjunct Professor of English at the University of Pennsylvania.

MY APPROACH to directing my plays is one that tries to do as little as possible. In other words, instead of solving problems by proliferation, by coming up with a million solutions to the small problems of a script, I try to disregard them and think that they will just sort of fade away anyway, as they have in my own experience, and try to get to what is the central issue of the play and how that can be put in a better perspective and stick with that. I also try to leave the subtext of the play in the subtext, where it belongs, and not to drag it out and over-elaborate it, which I think is one of the great mistakes that developmental processes sometimes make.

When I direct, what I want to know is whether or not the situation reaches out, grabs the audience, unifies them, and makes them one thing—interested in what's going on. If I can see that the audience is truly interested in what I've got going, then I'm happy. All I want to know is, does the central dramatic conception hold an audience? That's the only thing that I care about. I've had post-show discussions, and that's fine with me. I'm always interested in what people think about what they've seen, but that has a lot less effect upon me than the visceral sense in the room of a listening, fascinated audience.

I direct a lot of my plays in first productions, not because I really want to, but simply because so many times I have been unable to find directors who just get it. In other words, my plays are directed by very fine people, very good directors, who are extremely successful in directing other plays, but they just don't get how to go about making mine work. The main trouble I have with directors is convincing them what they don't have to do. They want to do so many things that are not only unnecessary but misleading. For example, there's a play of mine in which a man and a woman are having a fight. There's a lot of married tension. The director had the idea of a clock ticking. This was his contribution to the scene. Well, the ticking clock just made everything dead. You just listened to this goddamned clock ticking and the life of the fight and what was going on with the people died. If the director comes up with an idea that's not in the script, I don't care, as long as it works. But when it doesn't work, very often it's hard to dissuade a director from doing it anyway.

Most of the directors that I work well with I like and respect as people. Tom Bullard, who directed "Z" at the Actors Theatre of Louisville, described it very well: we were at this Mon-

tana conference and he said, "Well, what I do for the playwright, the way I want to work on a new play, I take whatever's
given me and we talk about the play, of course, and I stage
it. I get it up on its feet and then I get it into a state so that
the playwright can come and decide what's wrong with it."
Now that presumes a playwright who's able to look at a play
and say, "Yep, this is no good, I've got to change this," and
so on. But that's what he does, and that way he and I can
both go to work on the play. That's such a relief, instead of
a situation where it is decided before I have a chance to look
at it what's wrong with the play and what needs to be done.
Then you get into these endless arguments about this, this,
this, and this, which is very counterproductive.

I rewrite endlessly during a workshop production. One of
the things that you have to be careful about in directing your
own plays is to have a wary eye out for that playwright part
of you. The playwright's tendency is to solve all the problems
by rewriting. All problems do not need rewriting. Problems
can be solved other ways, through the acting, through staging,
through this, that, and the other. But most of the time, if you
have a cast that you like (and of course, 80 percent of everything is getting the actors that are right for the parts and that
you get along with), then you can, as you go along, just in-
stinctively do a lot. I do a great deal of changing, not terribly
radical, often simple things, but they make a great deal of
difference.

A good development sign is when things are being cut.
When actions and behavior are being added and elaborated,
but when lines are being cut. Where you get really nervous
is when somebody elaborates things that shouldn't be there
anyway. They elaborate transitions, they elaborate descriptions, they make everything explicit. This is a perfectly natural
human desire for input. Everybody wants to have a function,
and so the people who are trying to help come up with these
ideas, but very often they are nondramatic ideas. We should
see something happening on the stage, not be told about it.

Slowly I'm beginning to see the outlines of a kind of philosophy of theatre in my time. I'm sixty years old now, and I'm beginning slowly to see the outlines. I have watched input come from different sources. When I was a young man, there was the psychological realism of the Actors Studio (I was working there as a stage manager; then in the eighties I was part of the playwright/directors unit for some years). I watched how much the Actors Studio meant in changing the theatrical thinking of the country. But most of its effect went into film rather than the stage. Then in the sixties there was the whole advent of a different kind of theatre based on physical life, Grotowski and all of that, and the development of Meyerholdian directing. I've watched the changing of the spaces as the resident theatres moved from small spaces into the large theatres that they have now. I think that all of this has taken the theatre further and further away from its basic source, which is the behavior of human beings. I don't see quite enough room for an actor to come onstage and to be given the time and the means to become fascinating.

Now, there is nothing more boring than a person my age saying, "The theatre was wonderful when I was young." The theatre now is so much more. It is no doubt better. Actors are able to do all kinds of things better and the theatre is completely different from when I began to go to it avidly in the late fifties. But there is less and less room for the actors. And finally that bothers me. It seems to me that the directors and the designers, and the playwrights, too, are writing overly schematic plays, or plays that are very rigid about how they are done, that the actors are pushed offstage. They don't have time to explore.

MARSHALL MASON

Marshall W. Mason was the Founding Artistic Director of the Circle Repertory Company in New York for eighteen years, and then Guest Artistic Director of Los Angeles's Ahmanson Theatre in 1988.

He has been nominated for the Tony Award for best director five times for his Broadway productions of Jules Feiffer's *Knock, Knock,* Lanford Wilson's *Talley's Folly, Fifth of July,* and *Angels Fall,* and William M. Hoffman's *As Is.* Other Broadway productions include *Burn This, Gemini, Passion,* and *Murder at the Howard Johnson's.* Mason has received five OBIE Awards for best director for his Off-Broadway productions of *The Hot 1 Baltimore, Battle of Angels, The Mound Builders, Serenading Louie,* and *Knock, Knock.* His most recent work includes William Mastrosimone's *Sunshine* with Jennifer Jason Leigh, Jerome Lawrence and Robert E. Lee's *Whisper in the Mind* with E. G. Marshall and Michael York, and Lanford Wilson's *Redwood Curtain* at Seattle Rep, the Philadelphia Drama Guild, Old Globe Theatre, and on Broadway. Mason is the recipient of the Margo Jones Award, the Shubert Foundation Award, the Theatre World, a sixth OBIE Award for Lifetime Achievement, and the William Inge Festival Award for Lifetime Achievement. He is the past president of the Society of Stage Directors and Choreographers and a member of the Directors Guild of America.

WHEN WE first formed the writers' unit at Circle Rep we tried to determine whether *any* kind of workshop was of *any* value whatsoever to writers. Almost all our writers had participated in some kind of workshop previously and most of them agreed they're bullshit: writers sitting around and telling each other how they would have written the play if they had written it.

Several principles emerged from this meeting. Everyone agreed that hearing his or her work read aloud was really very helpful, so *that* became a cornerstone. We would have public readings because that seemed to help the playwrights. At Circle Rep we read a new play every Friday afternoon in order to get all the actors together once a week (as well as the writers) so we could share some kind of artistic experience. The Friday readings gave us a chance to experiment with the interaction between the acting company and the writer. Circle Rep was really unique because it was the only company of actors devoted to creating new plays.

Of course, at the same time, it gave us a chance to see each other's work and to evaluate new plays. We would read the play without regard to the performance, because it wasn't about the performance, it was really about the play. I would then conduct a critique.

Another thing generally agreed upon was that criticism was of little value unless it was specific to help the writer achieve his or her goals. In other words, if you're trying to write a mystery, it doesn't help at all for somebody to say, "Well, I didn't think it was funny." Because who says it has to be funny? If you're writing a mystery, that's what you're doing—I'm using very broad examples. So we decided that no criticism would be given unless it was specifically requested and that we would tailor all criticism to the needs of the writer involved. So after each Friday meeting the first thing that I did was to ask the writer, "What would you like us to comment on?" It could be as limited as, "I want you only to tell me the things you liked about it," because sometimes writers need encouragement and that's the most important thing. So that's one of the options: if you want us only to praise you, we'll tell you what we like about it and bite our tongue about what we didn't like. If you want only negative criticism, we'll tell you what we didn't like. Perhaps you want to know about the plot—how the plot was developed, how it was layered in, that sort of thing. If you want to talk about only the characters, we'll talk only about the characters: what we liked about them, what we didn't. Whatever the writer wanted us to talk about, that's what we talked about.

Many writers were too egocentric to take advantage of this. They said, "Oh, just say anything you like," which was counterproductive to what would help them specifically. When writers gave me that opening, I could be quite critical, because I have very high standards and I see no reason why a writer shouldn't be judged by the very best. So I start with Chekhov and Ibsen and Shakespeare and I try to evaluate the new work in terms of the highest possible standards. I could be quite harsh given the opportunity. Some writers would get their egos bruised and go away and lick their wounds. Writers will often say to you, "Tell me what you think of my play," and if you start to say something critical their eyes just glaze over and they don't even hear it. They *can't* hear it. So, I don't know that we were always successful at these public play readings. The writers who were clever enough to take us up on the opportunity to hear specific things really got something out of it.

That was our basic approach. Then the second level of development began when we found a play that we wanted to explore further. And if we found a play that we felt we might actually end up doing on our main stage, we would then go into a PIP [Play in Progress].

The PIP was generally rehearsed for a week, and then we would do two performances and then there would be another week for the writer to revise, based on audience response. After each performance, or presentation, we would ask the audience specifically to help us answer certain questions. For example, when we did *Fifth of July*, one of the things Lanford Wilson and I wanted to know was whether everybody could follow the nature of the relationships, because they are very unconventional. June and Shirley, for example, are mother and daughter, but they don't act like a typical mother and daughter: there is no father and June doesn't seem to have been married, so who are these people? John, we later learn, is the father, and his wife Gwen can't have children, so it's very complicated. It's not your usual sitcom where you can quickly identify the different relationships. So, one of the things we wanted to learn from our audience was: Do you follow it? Could you pick out what the relationships were? The audience had some difficulties understanding exactly what the relationships were, so clarification came into the play. Shirley would walk through the room and June would say, "Shirley. Stop walking around in that ridiculous outfit." And Kenny would then say, "Shirley, your *mother* is talking to you." And when Shirley would continue to ignore her, June would say, "Shirley, your *uncle* is talking to you." It's a laugh and works well and, at the same time, it clarifies what their relationships are.

When you have really specific questions like that, a general audience can be very helpful. It's very dangerous to say to an audience, "Just tell us what you thought." Immediately somebody will say, "I don't like this kind of play, I wish you did something else here," and so on. We don't allow the writers to defend themselves to the audience. The audience is not permitted to ask questions like: "Why did you do this?" We think the play should stand on its own and speak for itself. We tried to get the writer, instead of wanting to defend the work, to *listen*. It's a rare opportunity to get that kind of feedback in the American theatre, to get something that might actually help your play get better.

The writer then has a chance, during that week between performances, to do revisions. The actors come in for a brief rehearsal before the second weekend, the changes are put into the play, and on the second weekend there are two more performances for which the author has a chance to experiment with answers to the problems that arose during the first performance.

Now, the PIP process could vary in form, because it wasn't just for the writers (although that was the focus of it), it was also for the actors and directors. Many actors and directors really enjoyed the PIPs and there were no regulations as to how far the actors and directors could go, except that scenery was not encouraged. We performed in front of the set for whatever production was playing normally on stage. Sometimes the PIP productions could be quite elaborate, with special effects and actors learning lines, really just like a production, only without scenery. Other PIPs were simply readings. We did the very first presentation of *'Night Mother* by Marsha Norman, who was one of our writers at that time, and Bobo Lewis and Kathy Bates did a very simple reading. They entered and exited, but basically, they just sat there and read the script. They're such wonderful actors that they really made it come to life.

What we were able to give our writers more than anything else was outstanding actors, who could just jump in and make the play come alive as if it were a full production. That's a wonderful gift for the writer to receive.

How much direction and how much movement varied from one PIP to the next. We left it up to what the needs of the play dictated and how much the actors, directors, and writers wanted to explore the play's physical action. That's where the directors can really help. If one is totally prohibited from any staging as a director I would find that terribly frustrating. What am I supposed to do to help? Directors want to stage, we want to move the actors around, we want to explore the action, that's what our contribution is.

Then we discovered that we sometimes needed an even more simple outlet as well, so we came up with the "Extended Readings," the ERs. They were really defined as something to be read, with no staging involved. There was less rehearsal and there were fewer performances and it was just a chance to put a toe in.

So the overall program went something like this: every Friday there would be a reading of a new play. If we found something of interest we might put it into an ER, rehearse it a little bit, do a one-performance reading. If we found it more interesting and needed further exploration, we then put it into a PIP and rehearsed longer, staged it somewhat, and did performances with criticism. And if we really liked it then, we would either give it to another theatre (which happened with *'Night Mother* and *Mass Appeal*) or we would find something that really interacted well with our company and the project became a regular subscription production for us. This is the way *As Is* was developed from Friday reading to Broadway production.

When we do our readings—our developmental process— you have to understand that it really isn't entertainment.

That's not the goal of it. In any workshop situation I discourage applause. It really isn't about seeking that kind of approval or entertaining somebody, it's really about exploring the material.

I don't think all plays are equally well served by this. Certainly with very visual plays (I'm thinking of a couple of plays by Beckett, for example), you could imagine the concept by hearing the stage directions read, but it's hardly to achieve it as it would be if you actually produced the play. Some plays are more dependent on scenery and costumes and performance than others. But I think the theatre is essentially a medium of the spoken word. That's one of the ways that Circle Rep has been at the leadership of the American Theatre. Ten years before we started, theatre had drifted into nonverbal theatre—the theatre of Grotowski and the La Mama troupe, for example, were exploring the nonverbal aspects of theatre. Clearly, that kind of theatre wouldn't benefit much from our kind of process. But we were trying to get literature back into the theatre and to say: "There's nothing as glorious as the spoken word matched with dramatic action."

I think of directing as a Renaissance art form. By that I mean that you really have to be an expert about everything and that's what gives most directors such horrible personalities and why we're so arrogant. You have to know history and music and stagecraft obviously, apart from general cultural things. And you have to have passions, but leave yourself open to things that really matter. It's a matter of keeping yourself open to ideas that engender excitement and that your imagination responds to.

I have tried, over the years, to isolate a method that stimulates good directing. One thing I do is concentrate on scheduling: I break the play down into beats and I draw up a rehearsal schedule based on those beats and I plan the whole approach in terms of when we're going to be working on what, so that if I call an actor to a rehearsal, she knows she is going to work that day. You'd be surprised how few directors have anything as concrete as a schedule or a plan.

What we do in rehearsal is try to explore an artistic terrain. The words are a map, and the actor has to go through the experience of actually going there and following the course that is predicted by this map (the script). That actual experience is what acting is all about—the course of creativity. The important thing is that you've got to at least know and understand the map. So I think it is important to know the text before you start. As a director, I used to memorize the text just the way a conductor memorizes the score. A conductor wouldn't think of getting up and conducting a symphony without knowing that score thoroughly. Knowing the play thoroughly frees the imagination.

By having something to hold onto, you can let go. Through conscious choices you give yourself a ground on which to stand so that you can dream about flying.

JACK O'BRIEN

Jack O'Brien became artistic director of the Old Globe Theatre in 1981. Acclaimed for his numerous regional theatre, Off-Broadway, and Broadway credits, and for his direction of opera and musical comedy, O'Brien has delighted Old Globe audiences with a dozen provocative productions since his 1969 Shakespeare Festival debut with *The Comedy of Errors*. During 1991, O'Brien directed the world premiere of A. R. Gurney's *The Snow Ball* and George Kelly's *The Show Off*, which featured associate artist Sada Thompson. He also directed *The Snow Ball* in Hartford and Boston as well as the American premiere of Richard Nelson's *Two Shakespearean Actors* on Broadway (in January 1992.) During O'Brien's twenty-three-year association with the Globe his thirst for a new look at American classics has brought audiences revivals of Philip Barry's *Holiday*, George Kelly's *The Torch Bearers*, Thornton Wilder's *The Skin of Our Teeth*, which was televised live from the stage of the Old Globe as the 1983 season opener in the PBS *American Playhouse* series, and the musical *Damn Yankees*, which moved to Broadway and was nominated for a 1994 Tony Award. O'Brien's world premiere staging of Stephen Metcalf's *Emily* was named one of the ten best productions of 1986 by *Time* magazine. His 1988 world premiere staging of Gurney's *The Cocktail Hour* was similarly cited after moving directly from the Globe to Off-Broadway, where it enjoyed a highly successful ten-month run.

During the 1986–87 season, O'Brien revived (for Houston Grand Opera) his staging of George Gershwin's *Porgy and Bess*, which subsequently toured a consortium of fourteen American regional opera houses as well as Europe. On Broadway the original production garnered a Tony Award for most innovative revival and a Tony nomination for O'Brien as best director. O'Brien's opera and musical theatre credits include Peter Maxwell Davies's *The Lighthouse* for San Diego Opera, Mozart's *The Magic Flute* for San Francisco, Verdi's *Aida* for Houston Grand Opera, Kurt Weill's *Street Scene* for New York City Opera, and Puccini's *Tosca* for Santa Fe Opera. His television credits include *An Enemy of the People*, *I Never Sang for My Father*, *All My Sons*, and *Painting Churches* for *American Playhouse*. His production of *Street Scene* was televised on *Live from Lincoln Center*, his Broadway revival of *Most Happy Fella* was seen on *Great Performances*, and his staging of *The Good Doctor*, with Richard Chamberlain and Marsha Mason, was shown on PBS. O'Brien has also staged major productions at such theatres as the Ahmanson in Los Angeles, American Conservatory Theatre in San Francisco, Studio Arena in Buffalo, New York, and the St. Louis Repertory Theatre. He currently serves on the boards of the Theatre Communications Group and the National Fund for New American Plays.

As SOMEBODY who comes from the classical experience as much as anything else, I bring a kind of classical mentality to the work. I hope I'm thought of as a director as opposed to a "conceptivist," or "conceptualist," or however one wants to term that these days. By that I mean, I am keenly respectful of and aware of the writer himself and what he has put on the page. I begin with that premise. If the writer is dead, as in the case of Shakespeare, I spend an enormous amount of time trying to figure out exactly what it was he *said*, and then as a result, what he *means*, and finally what it is he *wants*. Those are three entirely different and distinct steps in terms of my preparation and my ability to visualize or dramatize the work.

When the writer is alive and with you, you have the first part, where you listen completely to the writer. You're in rehearsal, you're up in technical rehearsals, you're doing everything in your power to support the writer, to deliver the writer's vision, and to substantiate what the writer wants. Then you put that work, which is a collaboration of yours but serving the writer's vision, in front of an audience. Then you have another responsibility. That responsibility is not simply to what the writer wants, but to what the play *is*, because sometimes the play is different from what the writer wants or sees. The audience, which doesn't give a fat rat's ass what the writer wants, will tell you in no uncertain terms that they are bored, or they are confused, or they have now lost interest. They've ceased to be fascinated by what the writer originally wrote, or what the writer wanted, and they are hearing with a different set of ears. That is where the latter part of the work begins.

That's why writers like Steven Metcalf and Pete Gurney are enormously successful, because when the piece gets up, they now understand their responsibility to that audience and both those gentlemen know how to address the problem. With *The Cocktail Hour*, when we got it up, the reviews indicated that it was enchanting and fascinating, but that it copped out at the end, and we went to work on that. Pete came back from New York and worked a week with us, and continued to work on the telephone, and we're still making discoveries as to how to put those complicated expectations into a kind of realistic balance, so that the actors are served, the playwright is served, and ultimately the audience is served.

Most of us are attracted to pieces because we have something to say about them. Clearly in the case of *The Cocktail Hour*, I felt I knew that world. I grew up in that world. That's very similar to my own breeding and upbringing. So I felt a wealth of personal detail and experience that was applicable to his story. I responded to the climate. A writer may write a play. You may love the writer's work, you may be very, very appreciative of them, you may even have done their work before, but it doesn't speak to you. So the first part of it is this totally subjective response.

Then the second is practical. It's like chemistry. You sit down and have a cup of coffee or a glass of wine or just a talk with this writer and you know whether or not you mix. If you think the same kinds of things are funny, or you think that you offer something and the writer is excited by that vision, then there's every possibility that you'll have a happy and profitable working relationship. But like any other relationship, if you don't hit it off, you probably won't hit it off.

I start very much as an audience. I listen a lot. I listen to the play read and I try to have no hard and fast feelings about it. I have my suspicions about what will work and what won't and those are either corroborated or validated or in some sense denied by exposure with a reading. But basically that's what happens. I listen to the writer talk about it, I listen to what he thinks the play's about, I listen to the play as I read it over silently, or very often aloud. Sometimes, in the privacy of my boudoir as we say, I sit down and "act" the play. By that I just see what moves me as the characters reveal themselves, what choices occur to me as I read the material, and I store those things up in the back of my mind. I go through sometimes a series of readings of the material with other people, to hear what kinds of sounds they make, what kinds of things they do. It's a passive experience for me at first, and the less I say, and the less I respond, the better I find the ultimate results.

I find that the best thing for me to do in the first several weeks is to shut up, to say absolutely nothing, and to listen and listen and listen, in as many ways as I can, to the truth of the play, to its flaws, to why its flaws are substantiated or which begin to disappear after a while. Sometimes I just don't understand things. I understand the play, but I don't understand at all what that moment is about. The playwright will say, "That's what I meant," and you think, "Oh, of course, I never saw it." Or, "Oh, that could be readily achieved if we do this first." Or, "You need to tell me. Why doesn't he give a speech that says that's what he's going to do." Then we have that kind of innocent dialogue, which is just like hitting a tennis ball simply back and forth across the net just to see how the other person handles it. It's as simple as that.

The ideal circumstance is that the writer is with you for at least the first two weeks of rehearsal. In the first week you're still reading around the table, still discussing relationships, still discussing transitions, still uncovering the initial mystery of the play itself. Then in the second week they begin to get up and move, so that he gets to see the way the characters and the actors are beginning to grow and interpret and flesh out. Then he must go away. He must go away for two reasons. There's a very boring period when the actors are simply learning the play and it drives the writer absolutely bonkers, because they aren't performing, they don't understand, they aren't making the transitions, and they can't be very helpful to him. The other thing to be gained is a certain amount of objectivity. When he comes back, he can see it's moving in a healthy direction, or it's moving in a direction very foreign to his initial concept. Sometimes the director can't see that any longer, because you're so committed to the path upon which your actors are going that you want them to succeed in that way and in doing so you lose some of your own critical cynicism.

Certain writers will know specifically that they need to do something. Certainly in the case of both Steven and Pete, they have come to me and said, "I have to redo that moment, there's something wrong there." And I say "Oh," and they come back with a speech, and I think, "Oh, I had no idea

that's what you meant there." That's why they see it. I wouldn't
see that. But very often we do it together. Very often I'll make
suggestions, saying, "I think something's wrong there. She
shouldn't say that," or "That seems to be a remark he wouldn't
make," or, "Why did you use that particular word? It seems
so unlike him." Then they at least think about it, and they
either justify it to my satisfaction, or they change it. But it is
a relationship in that respect.

I do try to get my own way. If I can't get my own way, I'm
a gentleman about it. Sooner or later you're going to disagree.
There's a moment in [Steven Metcalf's] *White Linen* just now
where we're very much at odds, because I think it should be
staged a certain way, and the writers don't. The ink is all so
wet right now, that I can't really replace it with something
else because I don't think I have indicated where I think it
should go and I understand their objections, but their objections are somewhat unjustified in terms of where I will eventually go with that sequence. So I'm dragging my heels a little
bit, because I don't think I've proved what I want to do with
it and I think we've got to wait and see. However, it can easily
work the opposite way. When we come to a disagreement, I
make as eloquent a plea for what I want to happen as I can.
I am fully aware that I may be wrong, or I may be right for
what *I* want, but not for what *he* wants, or we may *both* be
right.

I'm very much a collaborator. I think that the contributions
that the designers and the actors make are invaluable. I don't
think this is a two-handed game of cards and I don't see all
the other people as supporting pawns. Very often an actor
with real intuition and insight can be infinitely more helpful
to the writer than I can, because he or she is coming from
an extremely personal and sometimes highly connected place
with that character and that character's history and development and sees things that I wouldn't see. That's equally true
of designers. Designers can make you or break you by the
way that they either call attention to themselves or that they

in some way illuminate things that even the writer didn't fully understand.

The luxury of being alone in a rehearsal room with a writer with whom you feel great affinity and connection and half a dozen or a dozen stunning actors who are there entertaining you every day is really one of the great thrills of a lifetime. I actively and quite honestly loathe the audience and resent them coming in and don't like one of them. I would prefer to rehearse for the rest of my life and I would like no one to see the work and that would make me very happy. Unfortunately, it doesn't work that way economically. So there comes a time when I put this gigantic mass of people between myself and the actual experience, both literally and figuratively. I sit in the back row, and they're all between me and the actors.

The acting begins to change, because the actors who were hanging on my every word for four weeks, and the writer who thought I was the most brilliant and incisive person in the whole world, will find out that there are a lot of other people who disagree with me, and that *this* is funny, not *that* at all, and they are very happy to serve that particular appetite.

I think there is a rightness to theatre that is indisputable. It is no longer a matter of ego, it's no longer a matter of vindication. The piece is either right or it isn't. If it's right, no amount of critical high-handedness will prevent it from reaching its audience. Because the audiences know what they want. If it is not right, no amount of justification by the writer or the director or even the actors will substantiate that.

I try to instill in the rehearsal process an openness in terms of the writing and the acting. We're all in this together, so it's not a matter of my way or your way, it's a matter of *its* way. *Its* way is what this is about. If you believe in the piece, believe in it enough to have done it in the first place, you must have been attracted to something of mutuality about it, of commonality about it, something that you and it share, and that's a roll of the dice, to be sure, but it's a pretty good roll if you listen to your instincts and intuitions.

Instinct and intuition are things that we are never taught to interpret or use, and yet as animals—and we are animals—they are basically the first line of defense. That's no less true intellectually than it is in terms of physicality. So quite frankly, if you keep that space, that response, pure and free, something can happen for you, but you've got to learn to listen to it.

We have to constantly remind ourselves that the word playwright is w-r-i-g-h-t, which does not mean scribe, but means *maker*, like a boatwright is a boat maker, and you don't make boats in a garret. You make them near the ocean where you can test them. If you build a good canoe, then you might build an outrigger. If you go on from an outrigger, then you might eventually make an ocean liner. That is exactly what happens with playwrights. They need to be around theatre, they need to know that it isn't a mystic personal process, or at least not entirely, and that they have to exchange with sometimes brilliant or aberrant talents equal or in excess of their own and accommodate them in order to make things happen. If you look at the history of Burbage's company, you realize there was this actor called Will Kemp, who played the clown parts, and pissed everybody off because he kept improvising. I have actors here who do this all the time. Clowns will always be a pain in the ass. But clowns are inevitable. So we must make peace with them. There's no use slapping the clown and saying, "You must behave!" If you want a clown, you have to take that into consideration.

I don't mean that one should have license to kill, but just that this is a practical symbiotic situation, which needs positivism and nourishing and practical experience. The more practical the experience is, if you're smart and if you're to the manor born, you'll figure it out and you'll get substantially better. Maybe you won't build your ocean liner all at once, but eventually you'll be in the ocean-lining business. That's where Neil Simon is. No one ever would have called his shows canoes. They accommodate groups of people who can go around the world in them. That's somebody who really knows how to do it. He knows how to fix it. He's a person who makes from his hands and his talents something that is really substantial. We can support it, but we can't replace it. If we're smart, we'll keep more of these people in the fabric of the theatre, not expecting them to produce a masterpiece every time. I think that you have to make a commitment and say to people like Pete Gurney or Steven Metcalf, "Yes, come on, we'll put it on." I may not do them all, but they should be done, because only by the actuality of that process does that writer get better.

LANFORD WILSON

Lanford Wilson was born in Lebanon, Missouri, in 1937. He began writing plays while working in Chicago as an artist in an advertising agency. In 1962 (on the fifth of July) Wilson moved to New York, where he became involved in the burgeoning Off-Off-Broadway theatre scene, which nurtured the talents of playwrights John Guare, Sam Shepard, Irene Fornes, and Terrence McNally, and produced Wilson's early successes *Home Free*, *The Madness of Lady Bright*, *Balm in Gilead*, and *The Rimers of Eldritch*. With his longtime director Marshall Mason, Wilson founded Circle Repertory Company in New York and has written numerous plays for Circle Rep since 1969, including *Lemon Sky*, *The Hot l Baltimore*, *The Mound Builders*, *Serenading Louie*, and the "Talley Trilogy"—*Fifth of July*, *Talley's Folly*, and *A Tale Told* (later revised as *Talley and Son*). In the 1980s Wilson wrote *Angels Fall* and *Burn This* and completed a translation of Chekhov's *The Three Sisters*, a task that took three years. (According to Wilson, "It only took Chekhov a year to write the damn thing, but he had the benefit of already knowing Russian.") Wilson received the Pulitzer Prize and the New York Drama Critics Circle Award for *Talley's Folly*, and OBIES for *The Mound Builders* and *Hot l Baltimore*. His latest play, *Redwood Curtain*, received initial productions at regional theatres in Seattle, Philadelphia, and San Diego, and moved to Broadway in 1993.

SCRIPT DEVELOPMENT at Circle Rep came into being through trying to provide what the playwright needs: I need to hear this from actors I wrote this for—or actors as close as possible to the type; I need to hear it with an audience and to ask questions of the audience. We wanted to do readings of plays to see if we wanted to produce them, to know if the play was really finished, if it was right for us. So very early on we started doing readings every Friday and having discussion as part of a play development program. We had all dropped out of the Actors Studio, which didn't consider it a success unless either the actor who had done the scene or the writer who had written the play was reduced to tears by the question and answer session. So we knew what *not* to do.

The Play in Progress [PIP] was for the theatre to see how well a particular script went with an audience. Then we found out that the writers learned a hell of a lot from that too. We started doing it for three performances in one week, then a week off for the writer to redo things while the actors were still together, and then perform again for another week with discussions after all performances.

From early on I realized that writing for the company, for specific people, helped me because of hearing that particular actor's voice and seeing that actor's body. One also hopes that you're challenging that actor. I never wrote what I thought that actor *was* in real life—I mean, what are they going to play? When you're writing for specific actors, they pick up the tone of the character real quick, or you tell them: "This gal's a big broad, tramps around, and she's drunk all the time." Okay, fine, they do that and it's what you've heard—the right characters in the right voice, and so the only thing that we're judging is the script: are your words right?

What I expect from actors is to just do it for me. I'm trying to see if my writing is working; if it's as lean as it can be and if it really says what I intended it to say, or if it's interesting. Sometimes I don't know what I intended to say—scenes don't say things to writers very often, they're just this wonderful scene down by the lake, that goes wrong. And you just see if there's any slack in it. Is it surprising? Is it entertaining ? Is

it interesting? Is it true? Is it right? Is it at all—pray God—
new, or have we all heard this five hundred times before?
That's what you're listening for.

I don't ask actors questions. Other writers do. Other writers
say: "If you were going to stay on, how would you go on,"
and have the actors improvise.

My director Marshall Mason has learned that until I'm
finished with the first draft he's to be very encouraging: "Oh,
wow, I can't wait to see how it comes out." And usually he's
very convincing. Then I get all finished and it's: "I never
understood what you were talking about with this religion
thing." And I say, "No, I'm not saying that." And he says,
"Well, that's what it means to me." And I go through the play
and try to find what he's talking about since I didn't intend
to say that.

Also, I have been reading scenes to him since the first little
piece, or if he's out of town he gets pages in the mail. So he
knows where it's going, he's familiar with the characters. Very
often, I've had actors read the scene to me fully six months
before the play is going to be put on, so they know the sort
of character they're playing. Usually they're paying attention
to what they're doing and they say, "That's much better," and
I say, "There's still something weird about it." Sometimes
Marshall heard these early readings and sometimes not. He
almost never commented (and neither did the actors) on what
was needed. I'd hear the scene and say, "Okay, Okay, well
that stinks," and then go off and redo it, hot on a scene or a
speech.

As far as Marshall's work is concerned, I have generally
read the play to him before we go into rehearsals, or I've
read so many of the scenes that he knows exactly who the
characters are and how I hear it. He knows what the play is,
though he comes to rehearsal with no preconceived idea about
what the play should look like.

Talley's Folly is a good one to talk about in terms of development. When I first wrote it, the character Matt had already

talked to Aunt Lottie and came down to see Sally knowing that she couldn't have children. And he knew that *he* didn't want children. So he knew that it was a perfect match. But he just couldn't say, "I don't want children anyway." He had to go down and somehow tell Sally how he came to decide that he wouldn't bring children into this world, which was very difficult for him. She wouldn't admit that she was in love with him because she thought she was damaged goods—she couldn't have children. So, his object was to go down there and beat A: "I love you," and B: "I can't have children" out of her.

We read that and everyone was saying, "Oh God, it's so wonderful, it's so great, it's so nice," and I was feeling so full of myself. And then Marshall said to me, "So he comes down there knowing what's wrong with her and just beats the shit out of her; where's the risk in that? It's all stacked on his side. What's the fun of seeing someone go down and beat the shit out of someone, especially if he's already been told by the Aunt that she's in love with him?"

Well, he called a meeting, just me and my dramaturg, and I went in with a real chip on my shoulder because I thought the play was finished, but within just a few minutes the bristle that all writers feel when people start talking about their play that hasn't been done yet was gone, and I was saying, "Interesting . . . interesting," and I was taking notes. So I rewrote it with Matt not knowing that Sally couldn't have children. And the play became—as it was for me anyway—about risk. The play in a sentence is: to get what you want you have to be willing to risk everything you've got.

So I rewrote it that way and I came in again and Marshall was really exhausted and said, "I haven't the strength to read it myself. Why don't we just sit down and read it now. . . . I'll read Matt."

Already I'm annoyed, right? I read Sally, he read Matt. I'm sitting there listening to this guy go on and on and on and on, and I'm saying "But Matt," "Oh, Matt," and so on. (And it still seems that way a little bit: it was the design of the characters.) But really, I felt my part was decidedly under-written. More than that, there was a moment as Sally when I wanted to say, "You son of a bitch . . . " He's telling the story of his life and he knows he has to do that and the only way he can tell it is in this fancy, odd, allegorical way. And she's very interested, saying, "Come on, and then what? And then what?" And, "Dammit, are you saying this or saying that? I don't understand." Then he comes out and is saying, "So, I decided from that that I would never bring children into the world." And I said to myself, "You son of a bitch. How dumb do you think I am? This whole story was set up as an excuse so you could say that you didn't want to have children. Who have you been talking to? How did you find out?" As Sally, I just felt so exposed and so angry. Of course, none of that was in the script.

We went on with the script and Marshall said, "Very very good, very good rewrite, much much much better." And I said, "No, no, no, no, I've got to go do something." And then I went off and I wrote—in five minutes—all of that: "I'm out of here. . . . forget it . . . real cute . . . who've you been talking to . . . why don't you go back to your files. . . . you're real good, real good, but I'm used to that, they're even better down here." All of that bit came out of that reading we had with me playing Sally.

I don't know if I'd have seen it if I hadn't read Sally. Maybe down the line I'd have seen it on the stage, just objectively, but to feel it subjectively is really great. You, the actor, know everything you want to say, you're right there, you've got a bunch of answers that the playwright hasn't given you.

If something like that happened in rehearsal and I heard an actor identify that moment with the same recognition that I had when I was reading Sally, it would be: "Stop the wheels!" I would go to Marshall and say: "You know she's got a great idea for a scene, I've got to go work," and he would say, "Terrific!"

It's never finished until it's finished: the script is in flux. Marshall will come up with some too, he'll say, "Oh, Lordy, I think she's got about six more lines here," or "You're not taking advantage of the fact that . . . " whatever, and you say, "Yeah . . . but I don't think I want to." Then he usually pressures me into it: "You still haven't written that scene with the thing in it, and I can't correct that scene until it's finished."

The Catholic thing in *Angels Fall* is another example. Marshall really thought that the priest was so goody-two-shoes and I did not think of him that way at all. I just meant him as an ordinary person who was really very wrong at the end, who was really very damaging. But I was so sick of the "drunk" Catholic priests and the "adulterous" Catholic priests all these Catholics were writing. I think it was a reaction to that one about the baby, oh Lordy, *Agnes of God*, I think it was a reaction to that. I was so sick of Catholics writing about Catholics that I said, "You know, I happen to know a couple of very nice priests, thank you, and I'm going to write one who actually believes in God. Wouldn't *that* be a whole new concept. And one who doesn't drink—already you're on fresh ground." So that's what I was trying to do. But Marshall thought it looked like "Catholic is right and if you're not Catholic you're wrong and you're going to go to hell," which, being a Methodist, he wasn't very happy with and which, being a Baptist, I wasn't very happy with either. So I had to beat out whatever it was that gave that idea, find the lines that said that, and find a different way of doing it. And also find where that character's flaws were—where he was wrong— and really hammer them home so it is perfectly clear that he has made a very bad move. And when Marshall saw that, then he said, "Okay, fine. Now it's just a person. It doesn't look like you're writing a credo."

I'll tell you what happened the first time I met Marshall, and it was just a very fortunate thing. I had rewritten *Home Free*. (He had seen the original production and I heard about it, but I hadn't met the famous Marshall Mason from the

Caffe Cino who had actually had a play done professionally—forget that it bombed, that doesn't matter. He got *paid* for it.) So he walked into the second production and saw it, and I said, "Isn't it so much better?" And he said, "No, I think you ruined it." That's the first thing he said to me: "No, I think you totally destroyed it." So, we didn't talk about *that* play anymore.

The next time I saw him—there was a group of us: Clavis Nelson (he had directed all of Clavis's plays), and me, and Joe Cino, and Joe Torre—and I had just finished *The Sand Castle*, and I read *The Sand Castle* to them after the Cino had closed at one in the morning or something. And Marshall said, "I want to direct that play, I must direct that play. It's the best original play I've ever heard." I said, "What original plays have you heard?" And Clavis said, "Well, all of *mine* for instance!" But Marshall was very much like that: "I don't care if it hurts, I'm going to say it." We were all very pure. Very idealistic.

So I said, "You can't direct it. I just finished this and I have *Balm in Gilead*, which is this huge, big mess and I want to see it put on first." And he said, "Well, let me read *Balm in Gilead*." And he came over to the house and he read *Balm in Gilead* and he finished it and said, "I think you need a very good director for this." And left! *That* was all he said. My roommate, Michael, came in and said, "What'd he say, what'd he say?" I said, "He hated it."

I didn't see Marshall for a couple of weeks. Michael ran into him and said, "Why do you hate *Balm in Gilead*? I think it's wonderful." And Marshall said, "I love it. I think it's the best play I've ever read. I told him he needed a very good director, doesn't he realize that that means *I* should direct it?"

In the meantime, I had given it to a guy from the Actors Studio who had never directed anything: a horrible, horrible little nerd of a person, a dancer, who was beginning to direct. So I met with him and he said, "Well, to begin with: you have two entertainers come out from right and two entertainers come out from left and meet in the center; *I* may not want to do that. Why should I want to do that? I may want all four from one side, I may want three and one, why do you do that?" And I didn't hear a word that he said after that. It was just that sort of thing through the whole script, and I'm going: "I don't give a shit what this guy thinks. That's irrelevant and I don't care if he wants to *fly* them in, *he's* not going to be the one who flies them in. He's not going to be the one to make the decision."

Then I met with Marshall and it was sort of like an audition. I hadn't told him I had met this other guy. And he said, "All right, let me tell you about your play." And he talked for about three hours. (He had read it three weeks earlier, *once*, in my uncorrected typed copy, full of spelling errors with stage directions scribbled at the side. Of course, we all had photographic memories back then.) First, he told me the whole milieu of the play: the whole "lower depths" of it and what I was trying to say with that. Then the business section: why this could easily have taken place on Wall Street—which I thought I had hidden cleverly. Then all the social ramifications and what the play meant to our contemporary society. Then, how it related to the Bible, and the original Bible verses that it's from. That took about an hour. He did a complete dissection of the entire text of the play and all its social ramifications.

Then he approached it technically: what I was doing with the figure of the circle in the play; how everything circles back; why they turn and why there's a round in it and why I called it "a round" specifically; how it starts and ends in the same place; and where I got that from the Bible verse like six lines above the other one. He discussed the entire technical design of the writing (which I thought was completely buried), where quotes had come from that were buried in the play, and so on. And that was that for about an hour. He said, "I like the way you did this and the way you did that, and I'm not quite sure how I'd go about getting the effect that you obviously want." Or, "I don't know whether it's worth trying to do that directorially, because really you were just writing it that way and I'm not sure if it should be produced in that way—it's just something you did for yourself." My mouth was dropping on the floor.

Then he gave me an hour lecture on behavior and acting and the sort of artistic experience it would be to go through the rehearsals of this play in order to present people with this true milieu. In other words, what the rehearsal process would be and how technically he would go about doing that. How he, as a director, would go about working on field trips and all that with the actors, just to prep them. And when he got finished I said, "When do we start?"

I think it's fair to say that he blew me totally out of the water. He knew the play as well as I did, and he had read it once! When someone knows your script like that, when someone tells you exactly what you've done, that's the one to direct your play. And if they say something else, they're not. I think writers should audition the directors and directors should be prepared to say exactly what they think this is, what it means, and how to go about achieving that. I think it's really necessary for a director to understand when he reads a script and to be able to tell the writer so that the writer can say, "Yup, that's what I meant." And if the director—as happens time and again—describes to you something you don't recognize at all, you know you're in trouble.

RECOMMENDED

READING

Anderson, Douglas. "The Dream Machine: Thirty Years of New Play Dramaturgy in America." *The Drama Review* 32:3 (Fall 1988): 55–84.

Ball, David. *Backwards and Forwards: A Technical Manual for Reading Plays.* Carbondale: Southern Illinois University Press, 1983.

Bartow, Arthur. *The Director's Voice: Twenty-one Interviews.* New York: Theatre Communications Group, 1988.

Cohen, Edward M. *Working on a New Play: A Play Development Handbook for Actors, Directors, Designers, and Playwrights.* New York: Prentice Hall, 1988.

The Dramatists Guild Newsletter. The Dramatists Guild, 234 W. 44th Street, New York, N.Y. 10036.

Dramatists Sourcebook. Theatre Communications Group (TCG), 355 Lexington Avenue, New York, N.Y. 10017.

Kowinski, William Severini. "The Play Looks Good on Paper—But Will It Fly?" *Smithsonian* 22:12 (Mar. 1992): 78–84.

Morrow, Lee Alan, and Frank Pike. *Creating Theatre: The Professionals' Approach to New Plays.* New York: Vintage Books, 1986.

Pike, Frank, and Thomas G. Dunn. *The Playwright's Handbook.* New York: New American Library, 1985.

The Playwright's Companion. Feedback Theatre Books and Prospero Press, P.O. Box 174, Brooklin, Maine 04616.

Sarvan, David. *In Their Own Words: Contemporary American Playwrights.* New York: Theatre Communications Group, 1988.

The Writer. 8 Arlington Street, Boston, Mass 02116.

INDEX

180 · Index

DAVID KAHN received his doctorate from the University of California, Berkeley. He is an associate professor at San Jose State University. He worked professionally as managing director of the Bay Area Playwrights Festival, cofounder and artistic director of Sierra Repertory Theatre, production manager of the Eureka Theatre Company of San Francisco, and literary manager/dramaturg of the San Jose Repertory Theatre. He was regional chair of the American College Theatre Festival Playwriting Awards Committee and served as a professional theatre site evaluator for the California Arts Council.

DONNA BREED received her doctorate from the University of Denver. She was a professor at California State University, Chico, where she headed the performance program. She worked as the director of script development for California on Stage, San Francisco, as conference director for the Bay Area Playwrights Festival, and as assistant to the literary director at the Eureka Theatre Company. She is coauthor with Susan Pate of *A Beginning Actor's Companion*.